NURSE FORTESCUE & DOCTOR PADDON

stories collected and retold by

DAVE PADDON

ISBN 978-1-997667-02-5

Published 2025 by Brack and Brine. Design, layout, and editing by Brack and Brine. Cover by Perfect Day.

This book includes text by Sheila (Fortescue) Paddon and William Anthony Paddon, with permission from the Paddon family. Portions of the text have previously been published in *Among the Deep Sea Fishers* (the official organ of the International Grenfell Association), *Them Days*, and *Inside Labrador*.

Direct inquiries regarding *Nurse Fortescue and Doctor Paddon* to:

Brack and Brine
PO Box 1713 Stn B
Happy Valley-Goose Bay, NL
A0P 1E0 Canada

www.brackandbrine.com

Library and Archives Canada Cataloguing in Publication

Title: Nurse Fortescue & Doctor Paddon / collected stories and retellings by Dave Paddon.

Other titles: Nurse Fortescue and Doctor Paddon

Names: Paddon, Dave, 1956- author

Description: Includes index.

Identifiers: Canadiana (print) 20250255693 | Canadiana (ebook) 20250260476 | ISBN 9781997667025 (softcover) | ISBN 9781997667032 (EPUB)

Subjects: LCSH: Paddon, Sheila. | LCSH: Paddon, W. A. (William Anthony) | LCSH: Nurses—Newfoundland and Labrador—Labrador—Biography. | LCSH: Physicians—Newfoundland and Labrador—Labrador—Biography. | LCSH: Missionaries, Medical—Newfoundland and Labrador—Labrador—Biography. | LCSH: Grenfell Labrador Medical Mission. | LCSH: Labrador (N.L.)—Description and travel. | LCGFT: Biographies.

Classification: LCC R464.A1 P33 2025 | DDC 610.92/27182—dc23

MIX
Paper | Supporting responsible forestry
FSC® C103567
FSC www.fsc.org

To my parents, who gave me life.
And to Kim, who has enriched it beyond measure.

CONTENTS

INTRODUCTION

This book is a collection of stories, letters, interviews and previously published accounts from and about my parents, both of whom lived lives scarcely comprehensible in the modern era. Two of the stories, "Liberator, A Gift From Above" and "Butter and Snow Housecall," were written by me based on oral accounts as well as United States Air Force accident records.

Tony Paddon was the son of Harry and Mina Paddon. They were doctor and nurse with Sir Wilfred Grenfell's medical mission and came to Labrador at his behest in 1912 to run a small medical outpost at Indian Harbour on the coast of Labrador. After an extremely busy summer tending to the needs of the schooner crews involved in the northern cod fishery, Harry and Mina were told to proceed 150 miles west to Mud Lake and set up another outpost in an abandoned lumber camp. Thus began a 27-year routine of winters in central Labrador and summers on the coast. In 1915 a small hospital was built in North West River, and the winter operation moved there from Mud Lake. Harry and Mina married in 1913 and subsequently had four sons. My father, Tony, was born in Indian Harbour and considered it and North West River the perfect locales in which to grow up.

Tony attended boarding school in the United States before going on to university and then medical college. Tragedy struck the family on Christmas Eve 1939 when Harry, worn out by 27 years of dog team trips, succumbed to peritonitis at the young age of 58. Tony was ready to return to Labrador and carry on his father's work, but Hitler had other ideas, and Tony signed up for the navy as soon as the ink was dry on his medical diploma. Initially he tried to enlist in the Royal Air Force, which had a recruiting office in New York. He had somehow found the time to acquire a pilot's licence and had collected a few flying hours in various types of light aircraft. The Royal Air Force was quite interested until it was revealed that Tony was a qualified doctor. No, they did not put doctors in airplanes but would take him as a Flight Surgeon if he was interested. After some reflection Tony decided that the Navy would be preferable after all, considering his love of the sea and his extensive time sailing in small hospital vessels with his father. I can only assume that the Royal Navy did not have a recruiting station in New York, and so he proceeded to the nearest one available: the Canadian Navy facility in Montreal. Perhaps he had an inkling that Newfoundland and Labrador would be part of Canada within the next decade.

Tony spent more time at sea than any other doctor in Canadian naval services and returned to Labrador as soon as the war was over, finishing his working career as Director of Northern Medicine for the Grenfell Mission or International Grenfell Association, as it became known in 1914. He died in 1995 at age 80.

Sheila Fortescue was from Essex, England and always dreamed of being a farmer, something which would have been quite radical at the time. In her late teens she was ploughing fields with Percheron draught horses as well as managing livestock and mucking out stables. When World War Two broke out on the day before her 19th birthday, she decided to train as a nurse and "do her bit." Her training took place during and after the Blitz, and on two occasions hospitals she was working in were struck by bombs. She very rarely talked about anyone being killed, often using the term "very badly hurt," and I believe that this was a euphemism to protect my siblings and me.

Sheila took midwifery training toward the end of the war and would go around bombed-out Leicester on a bicycle delivering babies. She was billeted in a condemned house with a family of very poor coal miners. The house had been damaged by bombing and had an outdoor latrine. Post-war Britain was a pretty discouraging place to live, so in 1949 she decided to go overseas with the Grenfell Mission and nursed in St. Anthony, Newfoundland, as well as Harrington on the Quebec North Shore and North West River, Labrador. In North West River she met Tony Paddon and "settled down to married life."

Tony published an autobiography, *Labrador Doctor: My Life with the Grenfell Mission*, towards the end of his life, and in 2007 it occurred to me that Sheila's life was also worthy of record if for no other reason than that Tony may not have had nearly as much to write about without her in his life. What you will read in this book are transcriptions of roughly five hours of recordings I made with her in that year as well as in 2012. I had finally convinced her that she was mistaken when she said, "nobody wants to hear that old stuff." Sheila died in 2018 at the age of 97.

I am blessed with 70 years of records and correspondence as well as medical reports, charts, surveys and notes. Some material was published in the Grenfell Mission's quarterly magazine *Among the Deep Sea Fishers* and some has never seen the light of day until now. For instance, only the 1946-7 dog team medical patrol was included in *Labrador Doctor*, but there are four other accounts which will leave the reader with a full appreciation of how difficult the work was before the arrival of an air ambulance in 1957.

Tony Paddon was a gifted storyteller, as was his father Harry. If the reader is interested, Harry's journal has been published under the title *The Labrador Memoir of Dr Harry Paddon, 1912-1938*. It is beautifully written in Edwardian English and will transport the reader to a time when medical work in Labrador was even more challenging.

I think many of us who have never experienced war are fascinated by what it does to those who have, and I believe that my parents' wartime activities had a direct bearing on what they did after 1945. The sense of being part of something which was bigger than oneself and which required one to consider the greater good seems at sharp odds with what we have today. There isn't much room for personal fulfillment and self-actualization during conflict, and any display of such sentiments would, I think, be frowned upon to say the least. I remember my mother talking about the war and reflecting that in some ways those years were the best of her life. "We were all in it together," she said, and I have an inkling of what she was getting at. As for my father, he talked very little about it, and when he did it was usually a funny anecdote. Apparently there are lots of those in war. One day, in response to some prodding by my brother for more details, he said, "Talk to your mother. She had a much more difficult war than I did."

I hope the reader will enjoy what is essentially a look at two lives lived in an era of wartime, as well as what might be called "frontier medicine" in the post-war years. Innovation and ingenuity were in constant demand as well as never-ending lobbying of various government departments, and there are reams of correspondence in 20 or so boxes now at The Rooms Provincial Archives in St. John's. I live about a minute away and have spent hours immersed in this material. It's a fascinating read, and my intention in this book is to make public my mother's memories as well as some of my father's material which was not included in his autobiography.

As these stories span several decades, genres (e.g. diaries, interviews, correspondence) and authors, language has been a tricky thing. Generally, I have attempted to keep things as they appear in the source with a few exceptions. All but the most common of acronyms are spelled out. Capitalization and punctuation have been standardized. The names of places and people have been standardized as much as possible. This leaves some room for interpretation for readers familiar with Labrador spelling conventions. The same place could be represented two or three different ways in Tony's papers. To make effective use of the list of people and places at the end, standardization to a point was necessary. On occasion, I define expressions in square brackets.

The reader will notice the use of the words "Eskimo" as well as "Inuit" in these pages, and it should be noted that the time period covered encompasses the transition from the use of the former to the use of the latter. Indeed, much of the correspondence in my grandfather's papers reveals that in the first few decades of the 20th century, both Inuit and Innu were often referred to as Indians. I have decided not to alter this language so that the reader can see how the change unfolded during my parents' lifetime.

I have laid out the stories in roughly chronological order so that the reader can see what Tony and Sheila were doing in their lives before they settled down together. I chose to end the accounts of my parents' lives at the point where they were no longer as remarkable in today's terms. That is not to say that life became humdrum for either Tony or Sheila. After retirement Tony became Lieutenant Governor of Newfoundland and Labrador, so far the only Labradorian to hold the post. The five-year term was filled with interesting work, and they both enjoyed it immensely.

It has become common these days for academics and intellectuals to question and criticize the attitudes of the personnel who worked for the Grenfell Mission. I have a few thoughts on the subject.

It is said that they had a sense of the superiority of Euro-Christian civilization, as expressed by an aloofness or at least a lack of friendliness. I think this may have been another manifestation of living through years of conflict in which you outrank or are outranked by everyone you come in contact with. I believe you also learn not to become too close with people who may, after all, be lost to the said conflict at any time. On two separate occasions during World War Two, the hospitals my mother was nursing in were hit by bombs. As I suggested earlier, Mum only ever talked about people being "badly hurt," but it's safe to assume that there were fatalities, perhaps many. After D-Day, she looked after the wounded who came back from the Normandy landings and subsequent invasion of Europe, and she got a first-hand look at what modern warfare can do to young bodies. On March 29, 1945, my father's ship was struck by a torpedo, and four men were lost, as well as 60 feet of the ship. Twelve days before that, his previous ship was sunk with the loss of about fifty men. After the war naval colleagues of my father were asked to go to one of the death camps as witnesses. They returned and talked about what they had seen. 70 million people were dead, and many Grenfell staffers had seen Euro-Christian civilization at its worst. Others were familiar with the horrors of the first World War. Some may have been involved in both. So, I think it is at least debatable as to whether they thought Euro-Christian civilization was all that superior. The modern perspective doesn't seem able to grasp or even consider this, and I am brought back to the first sentence of this introduction. It seems to me that the criticisms say as much about those who level them as they do about the people they are levelled at. Of course, the latter are no longer here to defend themselves.

PART I

SHEILA PADDON REMEMBERS

It took quite a lot of prodding to get Mum to sit down and talk to me about her memories. It was unnatural and uncomfortable for her to draw any attention to herself, and it was only my putting it in terms of "doing it for your grandkids" which finally persuaded her. The recordings were made on two separate occasions in 2007 and 2012, and she was much more receptive the second time. A gin and tonic seemed to help.

Although much has been written about World War Two, it seems to me that personal accounts of everyday life are perhaps the most important from the point of view of historical record. In 2025, the last few veterans are leaving us, and I have an uneasy feeling that the present crop of world leaders isn't so very interested in the past. Neither they nor the rest of us should ever be able to ask, "Why didn't anyone tell us?"

SITES OF SHEILA'S MEMORIES

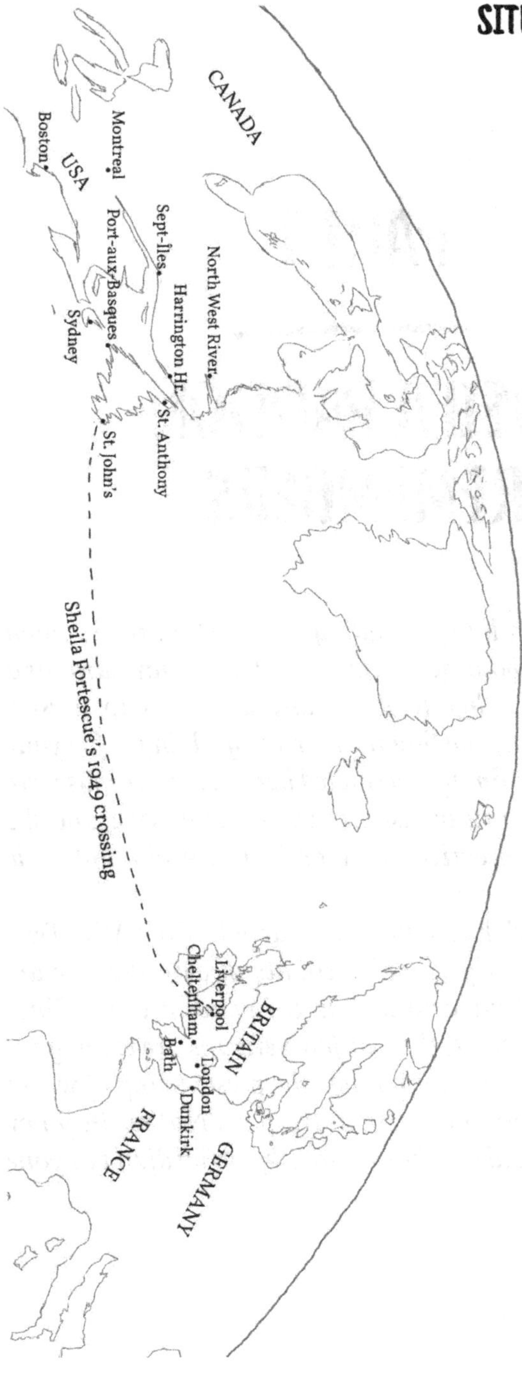

NURSE FORTESCUE REPORTS FOR DUTY

War was declared on September 3, 1939. I think it was a Sunday. I was at home, I remember. My father was there and one or two friends, and I believe my sister Valerie was there. We were told that there was to be a pronouncement by the prime minister at noon, so we waited for that. Mr. Chamberlain came on the radio and said, "We're now at war with Germany." Very soon after—a matter of minutes—the air raid siren sounded very loudly, and I'm sure several people thought, *well, here are the bombs,* immediately. We never really knew whether it was a mistake or it was a malfunction.

I remember leaving home soon after to go back to my farm where I was working. I was on the course of dairy farming at a farm nearby. So I went back, and a little while later I registered with the Women's Land Army, as it was called, for the war service.

Various things happened, but it transpired that a little later when I was at home one day—a day off, I imagine—I was talking to one of the four doctors who were billeted on us. In those days you were told that if you had any spare rooms, you must take in people from London to get them out of the city, which was obviously going to be bombed, out into the country, and in my home, we had four empty bedrooms. My father was told that he must take four expectant mothers, and he objected to this, because he was there all alone, and he didn't think he could manage four ladies who were expecting during an air raid. So, it was changed to four doctors. One day when I was home, I was talking to one of the doctors, and he said, "You really don't want to work on the land for the duration of this war. Why don't you come with me to my hospital? I'll show you around, and perhaps you'd like to become a nurse."

So, I did that. That was in October or November. I thought that this was a better idea, and I applied to the Women's Land Army to be released to go into nursing. It was the only service one could be a part of, apart from going into the Forces. They very reluctantly said, "very well," and I left the Land Army on December 31. I went to London to begin my training on January 1, 1940 at the Prince of Wales Hospital, which was in Tottenham in North London. This was the hospital where the doctor who was living at our house had taken me. He was a neurologist on staff there. I had an interview with a matron, and she said, "yes, you start January 1," which I did.

On the morning of the 1st, all the new "probationers" (as we were called) were lined up and told where to go and what to do and how to get our uniforms and how to behave and so on. You were on probation for three months, and if the matron considered that you were not suitable for nursing, you had to leave. If you could get through the first three months and you were approved, you could continue your training, which was for four years. It went very well, I must say. One thing I remember is we had our own bedrooms. I had been at boarding school for years and had to share bedrooms and dormitories. In this institution, we each had our own bedroom, which I thought was very good.

It was quite strict. I remember we were only allowed to have four possessions of our own on our little table in our bedroom. A hairbrush and a comb and something and something else. No more. However, we were given our uniform, which would be considered very peculiar nowadays. It came down almost to our ankles. Blue and white striped dresses with huge sleeves and starched collars, starched cuffs, and a big white apron. Black woollen stockings and black shoes and a peculiar little cap that we wore on our heads. And they dressed us up in all this—we new girls—and our names were read out as "Nurse So-and-so" and "Nurse So-and-so." Nurse Fortescue was to go to Alexander Ward.

It was a big old hospital named for the Prince of Wales, which would have been King Edward VII. It had long, long wards (26 beds), and I don't think very much had changed over the years in the layout. It was very strict, but quite kindly. On the first day of course, one had no idea what one was supposed to do. In charge of each ward there was a sister. The Sister was everything. She towered over the doctors. What she told the doctors to do, they did.

I won't go into it all, but it was "quite a change from mucking out the cows," as we used to say. It seemed to go along quite well. At first it was very quiet, but then the bombing started. They started bombing London, and we were in Tottenham and we became very busy. It was very complicated. There were certain wards that were to be kept empty for air raid casualties, but we had other patients we had to put in, and so on and so on. Finally, it became very familiar to us new nurses. We had to learn very quickly. Our hours on day duty, you went on at 8 in the morning and you had either 2 to 5 off in the afternoon, or you went off at 6 in the evening. So that was quite good. But we always had to come back if the air raid siren sounded. We also had to go to lectures. After you'd been on night duty all night and it was the following morning, it was quite difficult to study. However, the exams came regularly, and we were taught nursing, basically. Sometimes it hadn't changed much from Florence Nightingale's day, I think, but it was a good training.

And so I was there at the Prince of Wales and gradually went up to second year nurse and third year nurse and staff nurse, and I eventually became a sister. During that time, part of the hospital did receive a direct hit with a high explosive, but it wasn't on the wards. It was on the outpatients department and the x-ray. We were very fortunate that we weren't hit in the main hospital. At the bottom of the grounds of the hospital was a railway line, and it had anti-aircraft guns on the railway line. They ran them up and down during the air raids. The guns would be going off. I think they were probably trying to get these anti-aircraft guns when they hit us.

It was very busy. Of course, we did get one day off a month and then parts of a day, and it was quite exciting. We were very young, of course, and on a day off one could go into London and have a meal, such as they were. And if you had a boyfriend, well, of course you could meet your boyfriend, and sometimes you went to the theatre. The theatres were still playing. But it was always a race to get back to the hospital, and if you were late you were in very grave trouble.

We went on, and I made a lot of friends there, and I enjoyed it. Some girls didn't, but I enjoyed it very much. At one point we were sent away. Every now and then you would be sent away to a hospital that needed nurses for a particular reason. I think there were six of us who were sent to Hertfordshire to staff a hospital they'd opened for the Dunkirk wounded. They had built these Nissen huts—they were long huts and took 48 beds in each hut. They were fairly basic, but they were very necessary. Afterwards I think there was general confusion, because instead of going back to our own hospital when the Dunkirk people were transferred, some of us were sent to the local workhouse to nurse the inmates. I don't suppose you know what a workhouse was like, but if you've read any Dickens—it hadn't changed much since Dickens's day. They were very grim places, and they took in the old people who had nowhere to go at night. They were known as "tramps," and they would walk from one workhouse to another for a night's shelter. Otherwise they just slept under a hedge or by the road or in a field. They had nothing of their own. Remember, this was 1940. We were a bit surprised at being put in the workhouse during training, but one never asked any questions in those days.

So we stayed in the workhouse, I myself and a few others. Finally we thought we'd been forgotten, and we were very frightened really, but we wrote to the matron and suggested that perhaps we could come back to London now. She said, "certainly not," and, "stay where you are until you are told to return," and so we did, of course. However, eventually we did get back and finished our training. Then on June 6, 1944—D-Day, the invasion of France, which was a tremendous upheaval for everyone in Britain. For weeks beforehand, every road and field and farmyard had been full of troops and weapons. Anti-tank weapons and guns and tanks and huge trucks and thousands of men waiting, just waiting for the invasion. And of course everybody knew it was coming, but nobody knew when. And the days went by and the days went by, and then on June 6, 1944, it started.

I just have to tell you what the impression was, because it was as though the whole of Great Britain was moving out into the Channel. As though the land was moving, because all these hundreds and hundreds of troops and weaponry and tanks and so on seemed to start up at the same time and move south. They were all moving in the same direction, down to the ports, of course. At that time we were out in the country at this hospital at Bishop's Stortford, so they all went by us. Then the invasion started, and I was recalled to my hospital.

Just before I was recalled, I was told that it was not to be spoken of, but the invasion was very near, and I was to pack a small suitcase. I was not to tell my family or anyone else, and with five other nurses, I was to be in the hall at the hospital at six a.m. the day before D-Day, no questions asked. And so we six were taken in buses down to a place in Surrey, which was an old mental hospital which had been cleared—the patients had gone to Wales. It had 1,000 beds. We were told we were to prepare it for casualties, and that D-Day was the next day. So we did.

There were six nurses taken from all the hospitals in London and the southern counties to Banstead, which was the name of the hospital. We got it ready for the wounded. It was amazingly well organized. There were hundreds of doctors, there were medical students, there were surgeons and physicians. Everything you could possibly need. On D-Day plus two, we had the first convoy of wounded, and then we had a convoy every other night. They came off the beaches and were put in trains, I suppose, off Dover and on the coast, and they were brought up on trains, which came right through the hospital grounds. We only kept them for 24 hours, just did emergency work really. They were put back on the trains and taken away, I think most to Wales, to a safe area. We would have a night in between, in which we could tidy up and get ready for the next night. And so it went, and it worked quite well.

We were hit by a V1. They were the flying bombs that came across. They came in a steady stream, heading for London, and we were right in the flight path. They were overhead above Banstead. They had a name for it: "Bomb Alley," I think it was. They came over continuously, and they were frightening things. I think they were the most frightening things that we had to put up with during the war, the V1s. They made a horrible sound, a sort of grinding sound as they came. They weren't manned, of course. They were just flying bombs. The noise would stop, and there would be dead silence. If it stopped right above you, you knew it was coming down. They came down directly—they didn't glide down. However, most of them went over.

We had German prisoners there. Wounded. They didn't like their V1s at all. They would make a great fuss and say, "Was ist das?" They didn't like it at all, and they were very indignant, as a matter of fact. We told them it was their Führer's secret weapon. They didn't think much of that. They wanted to go to a safe area, somewhere safe. But of course, we told them they were staying right where they were, with the rest of us.

After three weeks, we did get hit. It was a very old hospital, what they called an insane asylum in the old days. It was a vast place. We had a hit, and it did a great deal of damage. I was on night duty. Very curious things happen during air raids. Each ward—which had about 80 beds in it—at the end, it had a kitchen where you were supposed to make hot tea and so forth for the patients, and 'round the end there was what was called a "blast wall." It was a sort of a brick wall around part of it, which was supposed to be bomb protection. We were told that if we thought we were going to be hit, we should go into the ward and get under one of the beds. I suppose it might be some sort of protection.

I had one Red Cross nurse with me, and my ward was almost empty, fortunately, because it was the night between convoys. We had about eight patients in there. So we got under the beds. It wasn't a direct hit, but it was very close. I think maybe the next ward or two were hit, but I just remember the noise of the thing coming down. I suppose I was knocked out, because I remember looking up, and there was the sky and the stars and all the smoke. It wasn't smoke. It was the remains of the roof. Everything looked shattered and so forth, but I was fine. I was all right. I called to my Red Cross nurse, but she didn't answer. I don't know where she was then.

The next thing I knew was one of the night sisters—the sisters of course were just like gods to us—you didn't speak to a sister unless she spoke to you—she was standing beside me when I crawled out. She was immaculate. She had a starched apron on, she had her huge cap with a little bow under the chin, and she just said, "Get up. Get up, Nurse." I got up, and she said, "Is your kitchen intact?" I said, "I don't know, Sister." She said, "Go and look and put your kettles on, because heavy rescue will be here immediately." She didn't say, "go and look at your patient," or, "where is your Red Cross nurse?" Just, "Put on your kettles. Get the water boiling for the tea." Which I did.

I wasn't hurt at all. My Red Cross nurse was alive, but she was very badly injured. She was right down the end of the 80-bed ward. I only had those few patients in, and only one man was killed. We were very lucky. That was the V1.

Then we all had to go back to our hospitals in London, because that hospital was bombed. I remember all the wiring was alive. If you picked up the telephone—we were told not to, but everything was quite alive. Something to do with electricity. We went back after that.

Strange things stay in your memory. I had been gone three weeks from my ward where I was Staff Nurse. It was a military ward—it was for the troops. I had suddenly disappeared on June 5 and reappeared three weeks later, and the men kept saying, "Where you been? Where you been?" Sort of, *Why weren't you here?* We weren't supposed to talk about it, so I didn't. I just said, "Oh, you know... away."

Anyway, it went on, and the war ended, and my training ended. I had an extra year—five years—because I had been ill quite a bit. If you missed a day of your four-year training, you had to make it up at the end, and altogether I had been away almost a year, off sick. Anyway, that was my nursing experience during the war.

Funnily enough, Victory in Europe Day isn't as vivid in my memory—well, perhaps it wouldn't be—as the time spent in Tottenham. By then I had finished my training, and I was training in midwifery in another hospital in London with my great friend Dorothy. We trained our general together, and we did our midwifery together at this hospital. That was a six-month course. You did it in two six-month periods: a year altogether. And VE Day came at that time.

There was, of course, great excitement. I think the routine, which was so strict, was relaxed a little bit, and those of us who could, did get into London. London was extraordinary. The whole world seemed to be in London, and it was noisy and quite weird. You could hardly get about. I don't really remember getting to London, but I remember the crowds and the music and the singing. And the lights came up. The lights were on. We hadn't seen the lights for so long. And of course tremendous celebrations from Buckingham Palace and the King and the Queen and Churchill. I don't remember seeing that. It was all in place at that time, and people were coming home—people you hadn't seen for years and years. Those that had survived were coming back, and you had news. It was an extraordinary time. And then it was over. That is how I remember it. I had to go back and finish my training, and the world settled down again. That is my only memory of VE Day.

The war with Japan—my brother was a prisoner of the Japanese in Hong Kong, and VJ Day came later. And for my family that was what mattered more than anything, because he and his wife and baby had survived, and they came back. My brother Tim. His real name was Trevor, but he was always called Tim from a little boy. He'd gone out to Hong Kong as one of the aides-de-camp to the Governor of Hong Kong, Sir Mark Young. Six months later the Japanese attacked, and they were all put into Stanley Camp. It was the camp for the civilians in Hong Kong, those that survived. The military went to another camp. They were there, and the baby was six months old, and the conditions were dreadful. There were thousands in the camp, and the conditions were dreadful, but they were young, and they were very fit and bright. Food rationing was mostly rice and a little fish occasionally, and not very good water to drink. And at one point they managed to speak to a guard in some fashion. My brother spoke Japanese, and they managed to communicate with this guard, and what happened was that Marjorie gave the guard her wedding ring in exchange for one egg. He gave her an egg, and she gave him her ring. She must have been absolutely delighted. By that time, I don't suppose it mattered about wedding rings. And they had this egg, and they cooked it for Adrian the baby. He had all of it, but he probably had it in very small mouthfuls.

Eventually they were liberated. I think it was the Americans who arrived first. Perhaps it was the British. They looked out, and they saw the ships coming in, and the guards just opened the gates and disappeared. They knew what was going to happen to them if they were caught. The prisoners just opened the gates and they walked out. Eventually they got back to Britain via New Zealand on a ship. We knew nothing. We knew Hong Kong had fallen on Christmas Eve of that year. We had one postcard in five years, I think it was, and we managed to have a postcard sent by the Red Cross. That was all that we heard until the liberation.

WARTIME LIFE

In 1940, when I started, the bombing began continuously. I can't remember the actual duration, but I remember very well that it was just part of one's life. In the hospitals—in mine, anyway, and I'm sure in all the London hospitals—you had these messages. There were three Alerts. There was a Green Alert when the bombers were on their way. Then there was an Orange Alert when they left the coast of France. I think that was right, because on Orange Alert, we'd have every empty bed in the hospital ready. We even had to put the hot water bottles in the beds. They were used in those days, on Orange. We all filled these hot water bottles and put them in the beds. At Red Alert, we could hear them coming, faintly. I can hear it now, as a matter of fact, very faintly. They were approaching London. Then after that, all the sirens went off for the whole city, and then the bombs would start. London was bombed incessantly for I don't know how long. You would hear it, but we only had that one major bomb in the outpatients and x-ray. Middlesex Hospital, a short way down the road, was bombed to bits. We were very fortunate, because we were in the East End of London, and they would come right over us. I think when you're young, and you have a job to do and discipline, it's not bad at all. You're all in it together. The hardest thing was for the old people and for the mothers with babies.

Of course, all the London underground stations were turned into air raid shelters. They were filled every night. The trains ran. They painted a white line down each platform, and as you got on or off each train you had to stay on the train side of the white line. The rest of the platform was taken up by people sheltering from the air raids. There were thousands and thousands of people in the underground stations, and they would bring their hot drinks and their bits of bedding and their mouth organ or something. It was like a little party down there, and, "Now you got my place. I had this place last night." You know? They were Londoners, and they were wonderful. At other places there were air raid shelters, and there was a rule that you must get everybody down into the air raid shelter, no matter what. Sometimes it was very difficult to get people down these winding staircases.

But at my hospital, as I said, we were taught what to do, how to do it, when to do it. The other thing I remember about it was night duty on the top ward of this big hospital. One of the top wards was the orthopaedic ward. Many fractures were up in frames attached to pulleys and ropes and so forth, and you had many patients lying in bed with both legs up in the air. They couldn't move, and we were told that you must never be out of sight to your patients. Your patients are everything to you. If you finish your reports and giving your drugs and medicines and so forth, you walk up and down. You walk up and down, and you do not sit down at your desk. Patients at the end of the ward cannot see you at your desk. So we walked up and down. But we were very young and very fit and cheerful.

We were frightened at times, but the discipline was so exactly right for us. For instance, when we left the hospital to walk across to where we slept and had our meals—"the nurses' home," as it was called—we always had to take our gas masks. The walk only took two minutes, but you had to have your gas mask, and you had to be wearing it properly, over one shoulder and under the other one. And you had to have your tin hat. You were in severe trouble if you were caught walking without your gas mask. That kind of thing which nowadays they would think of as absolute nonsense and silly, wasn't silly at all. I think that's what kept us all going. Maybe we've still got a bit of it left over.

Soon after the war started—perhaps immediately, I can't remember—rationing was brought in. There was food rationing, and there was clothing rationing as well. The food rationing came in very early, I'm sure. It was Lord Walton who organized that. It seemed the government was very well prepared for the onset of things like food rationing and so on. Each person was given a ration book. It was quite a small book with thick paper, pale yellow. It was printed in black print, I remember, and it was full of coupons, which were little pieces that you could pull off and hand in for certain goods.

However, having gone into hospital, everyone had to hand in their ration books, hand them in to the sister who was in charge of organizing the meals. She would have hundreds of these ration books in order to provide food for the nurses. I must say the food was quite adequate but very dull in hospital. One small thing I remember was that on

Wednesdays for supper, we had a plate of soup. Not very exciting soup, a sort of a thin brown soup, and an apple. And that was all you had for the evening.

When you were a new probationer, you were put in line in order of seniority. If someone started their training the day before you, she was senior to you and she stood in front of you. If someone had come after you, they stood behind you. It was very strict. The sisters who'd been there for years were treated as absolute—they were wonderful people, anyway. They didn't eat with the nurses. They had their own place to eat.

However, I just remember lining up for supper one Wednesday and shuffling along and finally getting up to this big, black stove. I was right at the tail end. It must have been my second day there. I held up my plate and the sister on duty scraped around in the bottom of this enormous pot with a ladle. She brought up a little bit of soup and something else, which she slapped down in my plate. She told me to, you know, "Get going." It was the floor cloth, the cloth they washed the floor with, and a little soup mixed with it. I sat and looked at it, I remember, and I was so overcome by all this seniority and discipline that I didn't quite know if I should say anything or not. Whoever sat next to me said, "What are you going to do?" I said, "I don't know." I was so hungry. I went back up, and the whole of the dining hall turned and looked at me and the sister. She said, "well, nurse, you'll have to be satisfied with your apple, won't you?" quite sweetly. I went back to my seat and had my apple.

We were issued with certain rations for the week. I think this was obligatory. They had to do this. So you were issued with your sugar ration and your butter ration and your jam ration. All the rest of the rationing per person was kept in the kitchen to feed us. So we sort of devised a method, each one of us, whereby we kept our rations for the week and hid them. I think you were supposed to produce a little pot, a little jar. Into it you would put your jam ration for the week. And then you produced a little dish for your butter ration and another little jar for your sugar ration. Well, this was a big, big problem, because when you were on duty you had to bring your rations with you because you went straight from the ward to the dining room. You couldn't go back to your room to get your sugar ration because you were going to have a cup of tea in the dining room. No, you went straight from the ward and straight back to the ward.

So you had to hide your ration. We all had hiding places, and we really got very cross and upset if someone else found one's ration. There wasn't many places to hide it on a big ward in a hospital, but we somehow managed, and I think somehow we were quite good to one another. If you looked behind something and you somehow found somebody's butter ration only half gone, it was very tempting to just scrape it into your ration, you know? But I think we were pretty good, really.

The butter ration was two ounces a week, and the jam ration seemed to be two spoonfuls. They would put two fair size spoonfuls in your bottle. The sugar ration, I think that was perhaps two ounces. Something like that. But the great problem was whether to enjoy your butter and your jam ration on the first two days, or to scrape it up for seven. Now there were the two-day people and the scrapers and scroungers and the rest who had a tiny little bit each day. This seemed to consume our waking hours. I'm afraid I made mine last. I couldn't bear the thought of dry bread at the end of the week.

You had one egg a week, but that was nothing to do with us. That went to the kitchens. For the civilian population, there was an egg and that was the ration: butter, jam and sugar. If you were a mother with children, you had the children's ration books, and there was so much meat per week and so much flour and rice and so on. But it was marvellously well done nutritionally, and nobody really suffered from rationing. There was enough, if you were sensible and careful and so on. We weren't short. And all babies had some sort of orange juice and iron supplement. The children during the war were very fit. They were in great shape and were taken care of. In hospital, there were times when we wished we had a little more.

Then there was clothing rationing, which was really quite funny. You could have a hat unrationed. You didn't need points. But you had points for clothing. A coat was 28 points, and that took most of a year's points. But you could have a hat, and you could have handkerchiefs, no points. So people made many of their clothes out of tablecloths and curtains and anything they had. And you'd see people walking around in a coat which was obviously made out of a good strong bedspread or something. It was fine—we were all in it together—but you had to consider your points very carefully, because they were very precious.

The only other thing I remember that was not on

points was candy. "Sweets," we called them. Sweets weren't on points. That was a good idea on behalf of the government.

I don't think anybody suffered from rationing. It was deadly dull. And it went on for—what, five years? Even when the war ended, we were still rationed. But the restaurants and the hotels tried so hard to make it interesting and thought up wonderful names for the food, which we all knew was just the same old food we had at home, and dressed it up with glamorous French names and so on. I don't remember any other rationing apart from food and clothing. I'm sure there were other things, but we all came through it quite fit and quite well.

In the hospital, the night nurses had to cook the breakfast for all the patients in the ward. When there was bacon, each man had one rasher of bacon, I remember. We had two little gas rings on which we had to cook for, sometimes, 26 patients. "And it must be hot, nurse!" We used to make porridge in a great pot, and on top of the pot we'd put the frying pan with the bacon in it, hoping it would warm it up a bit. Then when we moved the porridge over, we slapped it down on the porridge ring. And you had to boil the kettles as well.

Anyway, all went well most of the time. It was a great time, and I'm very lucky to be able to remember it, I think.

A funny thing happened at Banstead, which was the casualty clearing station where we had the first wounded back from D-Day. We had these enormous wards, 80 beds—40 beds each side. There was a locker by each bed, and it was very strictly controlled. It was military and it had to be done very correctly. In the bottom of each locker on the left-hand side was a cake of soap. In those days it was Lifebuoy soap, which was very harsh and smelled awful. It was used for washing your patients. It had to be at the bottom of the locker on the left-hand side, nowhere else.

I went on night duty at one point, and as I said this hospital was very old, an old mental hospital, and it had never been updated and there were huge cracks in the floorboards. At night, usually when everything had settled down and was quiet, the rats would come up. There weren't hundreds of rats—there was a rat here and a rat there and a rat somewhere. They'd come up through these cracks. You'd see their snouts come up, their noses and their heads. They'd come up, and they knew just what they had to do. They would go to these lockers and they would push the soap out of the locker onto the floor. Then they would push it to the crack in the floor, and they would ease it through. Sometimes they would stand the soap up on its end. They would ease the soap through the crack in the floor where they lived, and they would eat it.

Anyway, in the morning when the day sister came on, I had to go 'round each bed with her. Even the empty beds. She would see that they were made up correctly, just so, and pillows just so. "You must never put the opening of a pillowcase toward the door, Nurse." You learned that in your first week in hospital. I still don't do it. "Because it's untidy for somebody coming through the door. It's untidy." "Yes, Sister, yes." Anyway, she would say, "Where is the soap, Nurse? Locker number 21, locker number 37, no soap. Where is the soap, Nurse?" "The rats have taken it," I would say.

"Nurse, where is the soap?" "Well, the rats come out of the cracks at night, Sister, and they take it and they push it down through the floor." "Nurse, where is the soap?" I think she thought I was keeping it and I was making a little something on the side, selling it on the black market. It continued, and we had this little routine. Every morning she would say, "The soap. Nurse, the soap is gone." And I would say, "I can't help it, Sister. The rats come up, and I can't help it. They get in the bottom." I didn't say this, because you never spoke back to a sister, but I thought, *if they'd only have a little door on the bottom, the rats couldn't get in.* But, no, no. Anyway, soon after that, our V1 hit us, and rats and all went up, and soap and everything else.

BEGINNING WITH THE GRENFELL MISSION

After the war was over and things settled down a little, I was beginning to think that I would like to go overseas and work as a nurse for a time. I had thought about making enquiries about going to the Falkland Islands. I had heard that they were wanting nurses. But that really didn't come to anything much. The other place was the Kentucky Nursing Service in the States, but that was difficult because of all sorts of restrictions for entering the United States. The one thing that appealed so much about Kentucky was that they gave you a horse to ride, and you did your nursing from place to place on horseback.

After that, I began to think about going to Labrador with the Grenfell Mission. I had heard a great deal about the Grenfell Mission from a doctor I had met during the war who had worked in Labrador earlier, at a place called Mary's River on the coast. He was very insistent on the idea that if I was looking for somewhere to go, I should go to Labrador, because he thought I would like it and it would suit me very well.

In early 1949, I think it was about February, I went to London to the headquarters of the Grenfell Association of Great Britain and Ireland, which was in Victoria Street in London. The office there was run by Miss Seabrook, who had been there many years. I went up, and I had an appointment, and I said I'd like to go to Labrador. At least I thought I did. She asked me many questions, and the outcome was that she would send my particulars to the committee, and the committee would look at them. So I gave them my nursing experience and the examinations I had, my qualifications, and so on. She said, "I'll let you know."

I went home again, and I didn't hear anything for some time. In May, I heard from her and she said, yes, they needed a nurse at a place called St. Anthony in Newfoundland. They would like me to go out there as soon as arrangements could be made. There were one or two particulars I had to see to.

I would go as a volunteer. In those days you either signed on for four years straight, no vacation or holidays or anything like that, or you could go for six months as a volunteer, in which case you didn't receive any pay. If you went for the four-year contract, you were paid a small amount. I said no, no, I'd just go for six months. The one thing I do remember is I had to give the Grenfell Mission 40 pounds sterling before I left. I think this was meant to cover my expenses in St. Anthony as a volunteer. I wouldn't be paid.

I was also given a clothing list of things I should take to wear that would be suitable. Then a few more details. I was told that there would be a boat out of Liverpool on a certain date, sailing from Liverpool to St. John's in Newfoundland. The *SS Nova Scotia* or possibly the *SS Newfoundland.* They were the two vessels owned by the Furness Withy Company, and they sailed regularly from Liverpool to St. John's to

Halifax to Boston, round trip.

It all went quite well, and I went aboard the ship in Liverpool and set off for St. John's. I remember I shared a cabin with a girl from Newfoundland who had been training in London as a nurse. She came from Bell Island. The voyage took about seven days, I think. It was pretty rough, and I remember being pretty seasick. However, finally we arrived in St. John's. It became a little confusing after that, because I had been told in London that I would be met in St. John's on arrival by the secretary of the Grenfell Mission, who had her office in St. John's. She would meet me and take me to the hotel, and she would have arranged my passage to St. Anthony. However, it so happened that she wasn't there. In fact there wasn't anybody on the dock for my arrival. All the passengers went ashore and went home, wherever they were going, and I eventually found myself quite alone and wondering what I should do and where I should go. I didn't have any funds, and after some time I thought the best thing I could do was go back aboard the ship. I asked the purser if I could have my cabin for one night. He didn't like it very much, but he said yes, and so I went back to my cabin and I thought, *tomorrow Miss Garland will be on the dock, and all will be well.*

In the morning, a very tall gentleman came to my cabin. He asked me if I was Miss Fortescue. I was to go with him. I went ashore, and he took me to the Newfoundland Hotel. We went up to the desk. He didn't give me his name, but he seemed to be in charge, and he arranged for me to have a room at the hotel. Later I discovered that he was Doctor Cluny MacPherson, and he was very well known in St. John's.

I stayed at the hotel for some time, because the ship that was to take me to St. Anthony, the *SS Kyle*, was icebound outside St. Anthony. Although this was June, the season was very late. The ice was still in the Straits of Belle Isle, and the vessel was icebound. She couldn't move. There was no way of getting to St. Anthony until she came down to St. John's. However, I was very anxious to get to work, and after a few days, I was told that there was a small airplane flying to St. Anthony, and possibly I would be able to have a ride if I could find the pilot and ask him if he could take me. After making several enquiries, I found out that the pilot would be at the hotel at a certain time, and that he would be leaving the following day. I managed to contact him, and after some doubt on his part, he agreed that, very well, he would take me. He was going to fly to St. Anthony with a part for the fish plant there.

His instructions were that I was to be at a certain place at five in the morning the following day, and we would take off from a pond. Now when he said a "pond"—of course a pond in England is not very big, but in Newfoundland a pond can be a lake. It was called "Quidi Vidi" or "Qwida Vida,"I wasn't sure, but I was to be there. Those were my instructions.

I was there the next morning. It was a small airplane, and he had a very large piece of machinery in it. We took off, and we flew north most of the day. It was getting quite late and quite dark by the time we landed in a place called Roddickton. Earlier in the day, we were delayed, because he'd had to come down on Gander Lake to get some parts from Gander. I just waited by the side of the lake, and it was some time before he came back. He had a little trouble with one of the floats—it had sprung a leak. So that delayed us on our way north. However, we did arrive in Roddickton, on the east coast of the Northern Peninsula, and we obviously would have to stay there for the night, as it was dark by then.

He took me to the nursing station. There was a nurse at several stations along the coast, Grenfell Mission nurses. She had the station at Roddickton. She was alone there, and she'd been there many years. But she was full. She had no beds. So we left there, and the pilot took me to another house where I was to stay the night. He left, and I stayed the night at this house in Roddickton with this family there. It was quite an experience, really. There was a very small bedroom, but there was the bed and a chair and a bucket in the corner. And the good lady said, "Well, here you are. Stay here for the night." So I was about to lie down on the bed when a very large lady came in who was also going to stay the night in that same room, apparently. It worked out quite well. She had the bed, and I sat on the chair. I was very tired, and it didn't worry me very much, but outside in the night the dogs started to howl. I didn't know anything about these dogs, and it sounded like wolves to me. *But obviously they couldn't be wolves so close to the house,* I thought to myself.

All went well, and in the morning the pilot came for me and we set off very early for St. Anthony. After a time we approached St. Anthony, and looking down we could see the *Kyle* in the ice. There wasn't very much water to land. He was on floats and he had to land in the water. So he looked about for some time and found what I think he called a "small lead," a small bay near St. Anthony where he would bring the plane down, which he did very well. After a while, news must have got abroad that we were there, and eventually some people came out. They had a canoe and equipment to take us across the ice to the hospital at St. Anthony.

My arrival was a little unprecedented, I would say, because they had no idea when I was going to arrive. In fact, they thought I wouldn't arrive at all until the *Kyle* had been down to St. John's to pick me up to bring me back again. But here I was, and the head nurse was quite annoyed, I'm afraid. She said, "well, we didn't expect you yet," and, "how did you arrive?" and, "There isn't a room for you anyway." It was all rather tiresome, my arrival, or so it seemed, which was a bit of a disappointment, because I thought they'd been waiting for me and that I was needed. But that was all right. Finally I was taken up to Doctor Curtis's house. He was the superintendent, and he said that his wife would find a room for me, which she did very kindly. And so I arrived at St. Anthony for six months as a volunteer nurse and began working there.

There were just four nurses in those days. There was another nurse from England and two American girls. There were 100 beds and two doctors. We were very busy. There was one nurse on night duty and two nurses in the operating room and two nurses on the wards. There was no set off-duty, and it was a very busy time, but from the very first day I enjoyed every moment of it.

It was completely different from nursing in England, of course. The nursing wasn't any different, but the routine and life in general was something that I had never experienced before. Patients came in off the vessels. Off the *Kyle* and one or two other vessels. They came in from the coast in their own boats, long liners and so on. Patients would arrive at any time with all manner of conditions, and off-duty was very short. There were no days off. If there was time, you went off duty, but otherwise you worked all day, which was very good. I enjoyed it thoroughly. I was very fit and very interested. I think the difference from nursing as I had known it in England, in large London hospitals with strict routine, strict discipline, especially during the war, was here there was no seniority. There was only the two of you. You nursed as you had been taught, you did your best, and you dealt with every admission as it came.

There were a few differences in the nursing technique, as I found out after a few days, when I seemed to get into a lot of trouble with Doctor Curtis over my treatment of a certain patient. We had a man with an abdominal operation and very many stitches and drainage tubes. Well, I had been taught that on the fourth day, you took out so many stitches, and on the sixth day you took out so many more, and on the seventh day, you shortened the drainage tubes. This is how we did it in England. I'd been doing it for years, and so that's what I did. However, Doctor Curtis came to do his round and looked at the wound and found that the stitches had gone and the tubes had gone. He was very angry. Very, very angry. He said some very rude things about English nurses. We had quite a set to, and he sent for me later in the day in his office. I stood in front of him. He was an irascible old man, and he told me what he thought of me and what he thought of English nurses in general, and how it was a pity he couldn't have only American nurses, because they knew what they were doing and English nurses did not, and so on and so on. At the end of it he told me to go, so I went.

That evening, when he came in to do a round of patients, he came along and he had a huge bunch of pansies in his hand. And he thrust them at me and he said, "This is a small token of Anglo-American friendship." Then he was gone again. And after that we were the best of friends.

I stayed there in St. Anthony with various excursions to the outports and settlements in that vicinity where the Grenfell mission had nursing stations. The hospital ship *Maraval* would sail from one station to the next, visiting all the people along the coast, going ashore and seeing the children and anyone who was sick. Sometimes there was a delivery, and there would be one nurse aboard the *Maraval* and the other nurse would be left alone at the hospital. It was very exciting to be on board a ship, and she was a lovely little ship. Then there were times when one of the nurses would be ill, and we'd be down to three nurses. In fact one of the nurses I became very friendly with, one of the American girls named Ruth Norman, contracted tuberculosis while she was there. Tuberculosis was an absolute scourge, and there was no treatment to speak of, then. There were no tuberculosis drugs.

All we could do was put the patients out on the balconies so they were in the fresh air, where they were given as good a diet as possible. This girl became ill with tuberculosis and she was nursed there and later sent home to the States, where she entered a sanatorium. Then we were down to three nurses.

However, I thoroughly enjoyed it. It was a wonderful life. The people in St. Anthony were very good to us. They were very kindly people and uncomplaining, always uncomplaining. And life was quite hard. Diet was fair. I think they depended—and we depended—a great deal on local diet: fish and berries and so on. But life was hard then in '49. It wasn't hard for me, but it was hard for the people.

The summer went by, and the time came and I was to leave. June to December was the contract. But then there was the problem that since I wasn't paid, I had no money, and how was I to get back to England? I hadn't thought about it very thoroughly, and nobody else had thought about either. So I had my ticket from St. John's to Liverpool, and that was assured, but really nothing else. Finally I approached Doctor Curtis and suggested that I could go from St. Anthony to a place called Sydney aboard the freighter. Her name was *Nellie Cluett*, and she brought supplies to St. Anthony all through the summer, of various kinds. She made one last voyage in the winter and returned to Sydney, where she was berthed for the winter. I thought this was a good idea. If I could get aboard her, I could get as far as this place Sydney. I wasn't very sure where it was, but it was closer to St. John's, I thought.

Doctor Curtis wouldn't hear of it. He said it was ridiculous. I couldn't possibly go aboard the *Nellie Cluett*. It was beginning to snow, and it was a big, uncomfortable vessel, and the crew were four men. It was unsuitable, and no, no, no it couldn't be done. Then I said, what else could I do? My contract was up and I had to get home. Finally it was agreed that I should board the *Nellie Cluett* and get down to Sydney, where I would somehow make my way to St. John's.

So this is what happened. I left in November in a snowstorm. It was very cold. I said goodbye to everybody on the dock. The hospital staff and some of the patients and many of the people I had come to know and like so well were on the dock to say goodbye. I remember shaking hands with them all, and some of them looked a little worried. I think I was the least worried, but then, I didn't know what was ahead.

I boarded, and we sailed out of St. Anthony and down through the Straits of Belle Isle. It was very rough and very cold and very uncomfortable. The four crew members, Captain Iverson and his son and two others, were quite at home. They'd been at sea for years and years. They were remarkably good to me. They weren't used to having a young woman on board, particularly one who'd never been on such a vessel before. However, we went along and we got to Bonne Bay, where for some reason we stopped. They put the anchor down, and they couldn't go any further. This was something to do with the weather, I think. But there we rocked back and forth just off the coast at Bonne Bay for I think two or three days. I was very sick. Very sick. That seasickness where first, you don't want to die, and then you do want to die. I remember saying, couldn't they put me ashore? If I could get onto dry land, you know, it would be better. But no, they couldn't put me ashore. No one could go ashore. After a while, we continued down to North Sydney, and we all went ashore, and that was the end of the voyage, and they said goodbye to me.

I had a little money with me, I remember. I didn't know anybody, and I wasn't quite sure how I was going to get to St. John's, but I learned that there was a train from a place called Port-aux-Basques to

St. John's in Newfoundland, if I could get that far. I stayed in a hotel in Sydney, a rather small hotel, very dark, I remember. The good lady who led me to a bedroom said, "That's where Sir Wilfred Grenfell lay." I don't know if she meant that he lay there just passing through, or that he lay there because he was dead. She seemed to imply that he lay there for some time after he had died. However, that didn't worry me particularly. I was glad to be on dry land.

I discovered that I could get a ferry from Sydney to this place, Port-aux-Basques. I cannot remember how I did that or anything about it. Perhaps I borrowed some money. Somebody lent me some money or gave me some money. I can't remember that part of it at all. All I can remember now is arriving in Port-aux-Basques and being given a ticket to St. John's on the railway, which was known as the Newfie Bullet. And so I boarded the train and I remember sitting up. They had wooden seats, rather narrow wooden seats, which meant you sat bolt upright all the way. I think it took two days, but it might have been longer. It was a long time ago now.

I arrived in St. John's and thought, *well, now it's going to be easy,* because I had a ticket to England, and, *I shall be in Liverpool, and then I shall be home.* I went to the Grenfell Mission office on Water Street, saw Miss Garland there, and found that there was a letter there from Ruth Norman. She had written to say that she was in the tuberculosis sanatorium in Boston. I had promised to go and see her on my way back to England, if possible. She'd very much like to see me, and she hoped I would be able to come down and see her. I went up to the hotel and of course realized I didn't have any American money. I had very little money at all. However, I met a young man at the hotel who had been working at Hawke's Harbour, the whaling station, and he was on his way home to England. He very kindly suggested that he would lend me his American and Canadian dollars if it would be any help, and I would repay him in sterling when I got home. So I decided that I would go to Boston and see Ruth and managed to get some sort of a visa, which was necessary.

I went down to Boston. I arrived on Thanksgiving, or some sort of holiday. I went to the YWCA in Boston, and they said they could give me a room there for five dollars a night, so I took that. I remember very well spreading out my money on the bed, counting it out because I wasn't at all sure if it was going to last me and how I was going to manage. But all was well. On the opposite side of the street, there was a small restaurant where they sold hot dogs and things like that. I used to go over there and buy those, the first couple of days—and a banana. I seem to remember they had bananas.

Then I worked out just where Ruth was. I had the address. It was quite a long way, the other side of Boston. She was so pleased, so very pleased, and I was pleased that I had gone down there. I used to sit by her bed most of the day, and she was getting better. I do remember being very hungry and looking at her bowls of fruit and boxes of chocolate and cookies which she had, and how nice it would be if she would share them, which she did.

I think I was there about ten days altogether, and I was a little worried about money, but the one good thing was that I had a ticket to sail home either from Boston, Halifax, or St. John's. As long as I had that, I was all right.

Finally I said goodbye to Ruth. Just before leaving, I went to the Grenfell Mission office in Boston and found that there was a letter for me there from Doctor Curtis up in St. Anthony. He had told the secretary to give me fifty dollars, and the note said, "You will need this if you ever get to Boston." So there I was, very rich with fifty dollars, but of course I should have gone there first!

So I boarded the boat home—the Furness Withy boat, the same one I came over on, and arrived back in Liverpool. I made my way home, down to Essex and was back. My father wondered why I was a little later returning than I had said, but that was all right. I was there in time for Christmas.

BACK TO ENGLAND, THEN NORTH WEST RIVER

In 1950, I decided that I should finish my midwifery training. It was divided into two periods of six months each, and I had done the first six months. I decided that I should do the second period, and I applied to various schools. There was a vacancy in Leicester. My sister was living there at the time, and I was pleased about that. So I went down to Leicester and entered the training school there for part two midwifery. I remember it quite well, because it was so very different from nursing in St. Anthony the previous year. Once again I was back in England, with all the rules and regulations and strict discipline, and the fact that you were training as a midwife meant that you started right at the bottom again, with no seniority and no real responsibilities.

It was a six-month training. The first three months you spent in the maternity hospital going to lectures, attending antenatal clinics, and delivering babies under supervision. I think that was the first three months of the six-month training. The problem was that this was following the war, and there'd been a great deal of bombing in Leicestershire. Accommodation for midwives was in very short supply. However, the hospital was obligated to find you accommodation. I remember very well going to the office to be told where my billet would be, and was told that it was at a certain road at a certain address in the city. However, I was told that it wasn't very suitable. I had the temerity to enquire (which one never did in those days) just why it was not suitable, and they said, well, it had been condemned. They weren't putting nurses there because it had been condemned by the authorities as not suitable. But there was nowhere else, so, "Off you go."

I went to this house with my suitcase and things and it was not suitable. There was a great deal of coal mining on the outskirts of Leicester in those days, and this house belonged to a coal mining family. Father and two sons, all miners, and mother. It was very small, not very clean, and I had a little room there. It was so sparsely furnished that I remember sitting on my suitcase with the books on the bed, to study. There was a bathroom—there was no indoor plumbing—that was at the bottom of the garden, and it was used by the coal mining family. It was very uncomfortable.

When they came back from the mine, the miners would wash in the kitchen sink, which was a couple of feet away from the table where I had my meals when I was there. So it was not very pleasant. However, as they said, there was nowhere else. I could go to my sister's when I was off duty, but I couldn't sleep there.

The time went by, and the first three months were completed. In the second three months, you were outside the hospital on your own. You had to provide yourself with a bicycle, and they provided a bag which had all your necessary equipment in it for deliveries. And you were given a section. In your area of the city, you undertook to care for the mothers, which included going to the antenatal clinics and visiting them. When they went into labour, they delivered in the homes. They didn't go into hospital.

Quite often it seemed they delivered at night, and then the husband, or somebody in the family, would come and bang on the front door of the house where I was living and say that I was needed. So you took your bag and got your bicycle out and went to the house and stayed with the mother and delivered the baby. All was well, and you'd go back to your billet.

Leicester had been bombed during the war, and it was a very poor district that we looked after as pupil midwives. Some of the houses had been damaged by air raids. I can remember one or two things. You would push a bed against a wall to straighten it up perhaps and make things more convenient for the delivery, and one leg of the bed would go down in a hole because there was a hole in the floor. But that seemed very little consequence, really.

Some of the houses there were in very bad shape. Father of course would be there. Many of the couples would have several children, and the first thing you did was to tell Father to take the children out of the room and go out and sit on the stairs. They used to have these tenements where there were a lot of stairs, and it always seemed to me that Father and the children would sit on the stairs and wait until the new arrival had arrived and they could come in. Another thing I remember is that we wore this uniform: a navy blue coat with a small, round, navy blue cap with a badge. We were taught that you always took with you, to each house, a clean newspaper for the delivery. First thing you did at each house was spread out the newspaper and then take off your coat and fold it inside out, neatly, and place it on the newspaper. Place your cap on top of the coat and quickly fold up the newspaper and put it somewhere. This was what you did first of all, because of the possibility of vermin in the house. So you wrapped up your hat and coat so it was quite safe from anything that might arrive on it. We were very, very strictly trained in everything we did. And so you did your delivery.

You could call on Medical Aid. Medical Aid was a doctor, and there was a list (not a very long list) of conditions where you were to call Medical Aid, and the doctor was to come and take over. But the doctors were in very short supply, and they didn't much like going out in the middle of the night, so they would say, "You know exactly what to do, don't you? So you do it, and I'll come when I can." But quite often they didn't come, and so you did what you were trained to do, unless it was a very severe emergency, when you informed them that they must come immediately and to send the ambulance.

"Domiciliary midwifery," that was called—where they were domiciled in their homes. The next day you had to write up in detail exactly the nature of the delivery. You did that for the second three months of the training, and you did antenatal and postnatal clinics where you saw the mothers before and after. They were followed very carefully, and it was a very good system. You visited your postnatal mothers for, I think it was, four weeks. After that time, the public health nurses took over.

So that was the second part of midwifery, and then came the exam in London. That was all right.

I passed that, so I was a state-certified midwife, an SCM. So I felt that I could go back to Newfoundland, if I definitely made up my mind to.

At this point, I went to Cornwall to stay with my great friend Irenie Smart at Ty Brynn, which means "house on the hill" in Cornish.

Eventually I was asked to go back with the Grenfell Mission, to North West River this time to replace Miss Jean Smith, who had been there several years without any break at all. She was very well known on the coast as an excellent nurse, and she had a reputation for her hard work and efficiency. I remember being told in the London office that this was really a position of considerable responsibility that Miss Smith had filled so well for so long.

This time I flew back. There was now a flight from London landing in Goose Bay. I remember landing at Goose Bay in the night. There didn't seem to be any airport building such as one would expect, and I remember walking for some time. I came into the small graveyard which was situated at the end of the runway, and eventually I found one of the Air Force buildings on the base, where I went in and was given breakfast and a room to lie down in. I think they must have told me that there was nobody from the Grenfell Mission at North West River there at the time, but that eventually they would come for me. I was wakened later on by one of the RCMP, who told me to get up and go with him down to Happy Valley. I remember very well going down there in a vehicle. I suppose it was a jeep.

It was very bumpy, and I hit my head against the roof of this vehicle very hard. There seemed to be some sort of metal bar going across the roof. I remember it very well. However, it didn't do any damage, and I was taken down to the tiny nursing station in Happy Valley, which was run by the Mission. There was one nurse there, Annie Rhodes. I think there were just two beds for admissions, and she had a small room for herself and a small dispensary. She told me if I waited there, they would eventually send a boat for me, which, after some time, arrived with Mr. Jack Watts, who came ashore and told me they would take me back to North West River. He picked up my suitcase and we went aboard this motorboat and drove down to North West River.

I remember arriving at North West River, because the hospital ship *Maraval* was tied up at the wharf, and I had to step out of one boat and on to the other and cross that one to the wharf. It wasn't too difficult, but it seemed to stay in my mind.

I was taken up to the hospital, which faced the river. It was a small white building with green trim. It had an avenue of trees up to it and some grass and flowers, and it looked perfectly delightful. I was so happy to be there. Also I remember being greeted by Miss Smith, Nurse Jean Smith, at the top of the steps leading into the porch. She said she was pleased to see me, and that she wanted to tell me one or two things before we went inside. She had a list in her hand, and it was quite a long list of things to be done during the summer. It was a little bit intimidating, because the last thing on the list was that I was to make slip covers for the staff sitting room, out of blue denim. I wasn't sure what a slip cover was, nor blue denim, but it involved sewing, which I could not do at all. However, it just stayed in my mind. Then we went in, and she showed me my room. There were two bedrooms on the ground floor, and a sitting room, and behind that was a kitchen on one side with a little dispensary along the back and a waiting room.

The next thing I remember was the door at the back going into the dispensary opened. I think I was starting to unpack my things, and this doctor, who was Doctor Paddon, called to me and said, "Hello. Do you know how to suture?" And I said, yes, I did, and he said, "Well, come out here." So I went out, and he told me that this gentleman who was sitting there needed his scalp sutured. It all seemed to be a big joke. I remember it so well. They were both laughing. He told me that it was Wallace McLean, who had fallen off a ladder, which seemed to be very funny to them both, and he'd cut his head. Anyway this was a sort of private joke, it seemed to me. Doctor Paddon said, "well, you suture him up," and, "You'll find needles and thread here somewhere." And off he went. So I sutured up this gentleman, and he left, and I finished unpacking.

Miss Smith came in and sat down with me and explained a few things about how the hospital was run and that I would find anything I needed in the attic, such as the blue denim and extra linen. She said that the roof leaked, so I must watch carefully and see that the various pans and basins were put under the leaks. We were supposed to be getting a new hospital, but nobody knew when. She showed me 'round, and it was very full. The hospital was built for eight beds but I think there were more like sixteen in there, plus children's cots. She said, "If Doctor Paddon wants to operate, there is an operating table under the stairs. What you have to do is pull the stairs up. They're on a rope, and the stairs will lift up, and the table is under there, you see. I shall be leaving tomorrow, and this is your hospital." That was fine, and we had supper and went to bed.

In the night, I was woken by somebody in my room. Matches were being struck. I think we had lamps in our rooms. I'm not sure about that. The person in my room was, as we said in those days, one of the Indian people [Innu], who were camped across the river. He made me understand that I was needed. He went out, and I went to Miss Smith's bedroom and said, "There seems to be a man downstairs who wants me to go with him." I remember Miss Smith saying, "Very well. Well, go with him and take the black bag."

So I got dressed and went downstairs. He was there, and I went with him. We went down to the river, and he had a canoe. I'd never been in a canoe, but I managed to get in, and we set off. It was wonderful. It was moonlight. We went up the river, quite close to the shore, it seemed to me, and we seemed to be going away from the community. However, at North West River the current was very strong, and apparently one went up the river to cross over and then come down the other side. We came down the other side very fast, and then he stopped and I got out of the canoe. There were tents, and I just followed him to one of the tents. I had no idea really what it was all about, but I presumed somebody was ill. We went in the tent, but nobody really said anything, but people smiled. I remember the tent was full of people, and there were some dogs too, and everybody was sitting on the ground. I wasn't really sure why I was there, but then the old ladies who sat in a group smiled and pointed, and I realized there was a young woman in labour. She made no noise at all, and she was kneeling, and I'd never delivered a baby in the kneeling position. Also her husband was kneeling too, very close to her. In fact I think he had his arms around her. The baby was very near, and I didn't really have to do the delivery, but I was there when the baby was born.

Everybody smiled and laughed, and it was a very happy occasion. I looked after the mother and tidied her up and so forth, and it was a very happy tent full of people. After that it was all very simple, and she lay down and somebody gave her something to drink. They smiled at me and nodded, and then it was time to go home. We went back to the canoe and back up and across and back down the river. I think by that time it was nearly daylight.

Miss Smith came down all ready to leave and said, "What did they want?" And I said, "There was a delivery." "Oh yes," she said, and then, I remember so well, she said, "They didn't really need you, you know, they just wanted to see the new nurse. They've been waiting for the new nurse for quite a while. I've been here so long and they're quite excited about somebody else coming. Well, goodbye. I'll be back in the fall." Then she was gone, and this doctor appeared and said, "Well, I'm off now on the *Maraval*. I"ll be gone for several weeks. If you really need me, you can ask Jack Watts to get me on the radio telephone. "Oh," I said. He said, "you'll be fine," and then he was gone.

Shortly after that, Jack Watts arrived and said, "Well I don't know what he told you, but I'm not going to be here either. I'm going down to St. Anthony.

But you'll be all right." And off he went. So I had the hospital to myself. There was a cook, Jessie Lyall, and two aides: May Sooley, who became May Baikie, and the other was Phyllis Mucko. They came to work every day at the hospital, and we became friends. They were very good. Without them, I couldn't have managed at all.

The next day I realized that Miss Smith, Jack Watts, and Doctor Paddon had gone, and I needed to really begin to organize my time. It all went very well.

There were emergencies. I remember being called up to old Mrs. Blake, who had fallen down. I think she had fallen down some stairs, and she had fractured her elbow. It was broken quite badly, and I put that up in a splint which in my day (in training in London) was called an "aeroplane splint." It was a big splint at right angles and looked like the wing of an aeroplane. There were several other emergencies, but most of the work was routine work. All of the beds were always filled.

There were a few emergencies in outpatients, one of them being Gordon Goudie. He had had an accident when he was getting his wood in and managed to injure his wrist with an axe. I realized that the tendons had been severed, and I remembered that I had seen tendon repair in my training by the surgeons. I really didn't think I could undertake to repair tendons, but then decided that I should try to repair what I could, and I did eventually manage to suture the two ends of the tendons. Of course one end was in situ, but the other end was a little difficult to find. I did the best I could and splinted it and spent a lot of time wondering what Doctor Paddon would say when he got back, whether he'd be very annoyed. It was rather alarming. However, Mr. Goudie didn't seem to mind, and he went off home. I'm not sure if he ever had full use of that hand again or not, but I think he did quite well. Doctor Paddon came back eventually and looked at it, and I think he attended to it rather better than I had, and I think all was fairly well in the end. There were other problems, of course, but nothing I thought I couldn't handle fairly well, although the radio telephone was now silent because Mr. Watts had gone. Nobody else could use it until he came back eventually.

The summer went by, and I came to know the people very well. I was extremely happy. I enjoyed every day. It was so different from working in England. I was so thankful that I had had such a good training in wartime in England, and I felt that I could handle the situation fairly well.

The summer went by, and Doctor Paddon came back, and it was such a busy time. There were all sorts of difficulties in maintenance in that old hospital, apart from the roof leaking. We burned wood in a huge furnace in the basement, and the summer volunteers (the WOPs, which stood for "without pay") came in mostly from the United States. They worked all summer, mostly at the head of the lake. They brought wood down for the winter and stacked it in huge piles. There was also one girl who came up from New York, and she was to help me with the running of the hospital. She was excellent and a very nice girl. She didn't mind what she did, and she was a tremendous asset. She would go down to the homes where people were sick and nurse them in their homes and also help with all the work in the hospital.

In those days, there was just one nurse and a volunteer. We also had a barn. I think it was six cows in the barn, and a bull. We had chickens, and we had pigs and wonderful vegetable gardens. Also there were some children in the dormitories. Most of the children had gone home for the summer. They came down for schooling at North West River, and they started to come back at the end of August for school in September, though some stayed year-round. There were various illnesses and accidents with the children, and they were looked after in the dormitories. There was the United Church and the minister and his wife, who had been there for a very long time: Reverend Burry [Lester Leeland Burry] and his wife.

I got to know everyone in the village, and it was a very happy place with a very straightforward, simple way of life. The Indian people who lived across the river would leave in the fall to go back into the country. They would take down their tents almost overnight and collect up any patient that was in the hospital. They wouldn't go in the country and leave anyone behind. Nobody had told me that, and I had a little boy in the hospital who was only about five, and he had a very severe dog bite in the front of his leg. Doctor Paddon had taken a skin graft from his side, and we applied this skin graft to the leg and hoped it would take. It was very difficult, because skin grafts are difficult, and to make them "take" (as it was called) takes a great deal of careful nursing. I had looked after the little boy fairly well, I had thought, until the day came when his father came to the hospital, picked him up and walked down the stairs with him. This worried me dreadfully, and I can remember running after him down the stairs and saying, "No, no, no, don't take him. You mustn't take him!" I protested very loudly to no effect. His father just walked out the front door and went off across the river. I remember thinking, "Whatever will Doctor Paddon say?" I remember thinking he would be very annoyed at me for having allowed the child to be taken.

I needn't have worried, because when he got back, I said, "I'm very much afraid that this little boy was taken by his father, and they've all gone from across the river and he's gone, too," and I remember Doctor Paddon saying, "Oh that's all right. They would take him, of course. Actually, when they come back next year, you'll find that that has healed completely, far better than we could have done." And so it was. They had used their own methods, and it had taken. It was perfect, no infection.

So it went on. That was the life, and I thought it really was the best time of my life. However, the winter was approaching. I was only supposed to be there for six months, and Miss Smith would be back. Eventually she returned, and my time there was up. I remember saying goodbye to everybody, and a lot of them were saying, "Where you going? Where you going, Miss?"

During this time in the summer, Doctor Paddon and I realized we enjoyed being together and working together. We understood each other very well, and although we were always so busy and the work came first, we were very comfortable in each other's company, and we were beginning to be very fond of one another. This was a factor, but it didn't make any difference, as I was going to Harrington Harbour.

This was in my contract. Miss Smith had returned, and therefore it was time for me to go.

The Harrington contract was for six months. I believe that I left North West River in October, perhaps the end of October. It was getting cold and wintry, and it was time to be moving on. I had to get to Harrington by freeze-up, as I was going by boat along the St. Lawrence, and the last boat would be leaving before too long. I went up to Goose Bay with Doctor Paddon. Although it's hard to imagine now, plans were not made for the staff ahead of time. It was left to the staff to arrange their transport to wherever they were going, and as far as the cost goes, they would probably be reimbursed eventually, but not beforehand.

I remember waiting about at Goose Bay for some time, and Doctor Paddon as I'm still calling him—Tony—was none the wiser as to how I should travel to Harrington. However, he had to return to North West River. We said goodbye at Goose Bay, I remember, outside one of the hangars there. He said he hoped all would go well, and so we parted, intending to keep in touch.

I forget the actual details of the next day or two, but eventually there was an aeroplane flying to Montreal. The pilot, who was taking the plane down by himself, had heard that I needed to be taken to Seven Islands. He suggested that I go with him, and he would take me there. He would stop just long enough for me to get off, and then he would go on. So I flew with him to Seven Islands [Sept-Îles]. This was 1950 or '51, and they were just starting the construction for a railway into the interior of Labrador. I don't think they had begun the work, but there was an enormous workforce there and much activity. It was very remote. I remember being left there and being told that there was a hotel of sorts. Mostly everybody there was French, and I don't think I saw a single other woman there until I got to this small hotel.

There was a French woman there who said that it was very unusual for me to be there, but that she could provide a room for the night. The boat to Blanc Sablon would arrive soon, but nobody was quite sure when. I must say, I wasn't too comfortable being there. I suppose it was because there was very little English spoken. There were no other women, and I knew that if I did not board that boat, which was the last of the season, I would be there for the winter, which was a very alarming thought. I can remember sitting in this little bedroom and feeling very uncertain. I was making a piece of embroidery for my sister, which I wasn't very good at. I can remember unpacking it and sitting there and stitching and trying to concentrate on this piece of work and not to think about my surroundings or my future, and being quite anxious, very anxious. There was a great deal of noise in this little place. It was all these French speaking men who were working there, and I can remember feeling really quite anxious.

HARRINGTON HARBOUR

It is now late October 1951. I stayed overnight in Seven Islands in this small hotel, waiting for this boat. The following day I enquired as to when the boat would be in, but they weren't at all sure. I had to get to Harrington on that boat, as it was the last of the season. I spent most of the day on the dock at Seven Islands, and eventually the boat arrived. She was the vessel that serviced all the communities along the North Shore as far as Blanc Sablon. She was very old and not very clean. However, I cheered up because she had arrived, and I went aboard.

There were only two other passengers. There was one young woman and Bishop Scheffer [Lionel Scheffer], the Roman Catholic bishop. He was visiting the communities along the coast. So I made my way to Harrington. She was very slow, I remember, because she stopped so often. I did go ashore once. This very kindly bishop invited me to accompany him at Havre-Saint-Pierre, where there was a convent. I was delighted to leave the boat for a while and go to the convent with him. The nuns were so kindly, and I was allowed to have a bath. We had a meal with them, and then we made our way along the coast until I reached Harrington Harbour.

It was an isolated island just off the coast, if I remember. I think I'm right in saying that. The Grenfell Mission had had a hospital there for years, and it had been replaced by a modern building, I think about a year before I arrived there, about 1950, I suppose.

It was very bleak and very cold. Doctor Hodd [Donald Gordon Hodd] had been the doctor there for years, and he met me on the dock. I remember he said, "Thank God you've come, because we are without a nurse." There had been two nurses, but they'd left, and now there was no nurse. There were many patients—the hospital was full. We walked up to it, and he showed me around. It was quite a large hospital for such a little place. The only staff were two girls from Harrington who assisted as aides, and there was a cook and I think one other person. The nurses had gone. There had been a dentist, but she also had been taken out because she'd had a breakdown. Everything was new, and I remember the dental office was in a terrible state—teeth on the floor and swabs everywhere. She had had a mental breakdown, and she'd been taken out by helicopter.

I think all the beds were full. Doctor Hodd said, "You'll manage, won't you?" I said yes, and he said I would also have to do the inventory of all the drugs. It was due at St. Anthony. He said that in 24 hours, he had to leave on his dog team trip. So it was busy. We did the inventory, and he left. There were two tuberculosis wards with active tuberculosis patients, and there were many other wards. Then there were the outpatients who came every day. I didn't quite know how I would do day duty and night duty. The two girls were a very great help during the day, but they wouldn't come upstairs to the wards after dark, so I didn't have them in the evenings.

Things went along, and a housekeeper came—

Miss Dumont—a French Canadian, I remember. Then a volunteer came, but she was supposed to look after the handicrafts, she told me, and she wouldn't have anything to do with the hospital. But she was another pair of hands in an emergency.

As I said, the hospital was new and in very good shape and very well-equipped, really. As I remember it, there were 24 or perhaps 26 beds. There was a good deal of open tuberculosis in those days and not too much treatment. Apart from the inpatients, there was this large outpatient clinic downstairs and a casualty department downstairs, as well as the dental office, which after I'd cleaned it up, I didn't go near. I started in, and in a way, it was quite exciting to have a hospital all to myself, with perhaps 26 patients.

A lot of them spoke French only, which was a little difficult, but the two aides spoke English. I set up a routine of nursing. Also, Doctor Hodd had told me just before he left that there were several patients in the community who have different drugs daily, or injections, and I would have to fit that in as well. I well remember that, because it started to snow and continued to snow. It was a very strange place, because it was very rocky with some sort of stubby grass and a few short trees and bushes, and it had ravines in it, very deep ditches. There were little wooden bridges over most of them, but after the snow fell you couldn't really see where you were in relation to these sudden ravines. I couldn't quite see where all the bridges were, and it was easy to drop down into one of these deep ditches.

I remember I used to visit the outpatients in the evening at about seven, which was the only time I could get away from the hospital, and then of course it was dark. It was quite extraordinary to go around the island and in and out of the houses trying to find the bridges and stumbling about with this fairly heavy bag, but I think it all went quite well.

The hospital was quite busy. Doctor Hodd was away for about four or five weeks. Then he would come back. We would go around the patients, and we would discuss them and so on. A lot of it was straightforward nursing, but there were difficulties, and at ten p.m. the lights would be switched off all through the hospital. It was something to do with the generators. We didn't have lights after ten. And so I remember having a hurricane lamp—it was rather like going back to the war—these big hurricane lamps which you lit and carried around. You could place one on the table at the end of the bed and attend to a patient.

It wasn't so easy when someone was having a baby and you just had a hurricane lamp at the end of the bed. It never seemed to shine the light just where you needed it, but I had delivered so many babies in various circumstances, and most of them were straightforward, although now and again they weren't. But the patients expected it. It wasn't really a problem to them, and it wasn't a problem to me. Perhaps I was just fortunate, but all went well. The most difficult case that I had—there were two. One was a young man with a gunshot wound in his shoulder. He had been in a boat with another man, perhaps they were hunting, and his friend brought him in with this wound in the shoulder. I think it was through the joint, and it extended to his back. He was in a very bad way.

I did all I could for him. He was young and very strong and fit. Otherwise, he wouldn't have lived. I remember trying to get through to St. Anthony on the radio telephone St. Anthony had the nearest doctor, but of course it was across the Straits of Belle Isle. I could only get a message to Flowers Cove. From there it would be forwarded to St. Anthony. If you really needed a doctor desperately, then this is what you would do, and I did. I remember getting in touch with Miss Durley, who had been there for years and years. She must have been there 40 years, I think. She was an English nurse.

I well remember calling Flowers Cove. Each station had a number, a code, and you hoped you would get through. I did get through to Miss Durley. I remember saying, "This is Harrington. This is Harrington calling. This is urgent." I remember Miss Durley answering and saying, "Oh, hello. Do you know my cat has just had kittens. Would you like one over there?" I said, "Miss Durley, this is Harrington, and this is urgent. I have a gunshot wound. Could you put me through to Doctor Thomas or one of the doctors at St. Anthony?" "Oh, yes," she said, "I'll try to do that."

Eventually I did get through, and Doctor Thomas came on and said, "What is it?" I said, "I have a gunshot wound in the shoulder." He said, "Clean it out." I said I had, and he said, "How much antibiotic do you have?" It was sulphonamides in those days. He said to pack it with sulphonamides and give anti-tetanus. "I've done that," I said. "What else do I do?" He said there wasn't much more to be done, but to just nurse him. "I'll keep in touch," he said. Anyway, I nursed him and nursed him, and I nursed him so much that he had to get better.

About three days later, I had his bed near the station where I sat. About three days later I heard this sound. I had in the back of mind, remembering stories of the First World War, how some gunshot wounds contracted gas gangrene. If this happens they get a condition called crepitus, which is gas bubbles under the skin and into the muscle, and it's extremely dangerous. I could hardly believe my ears. I remember sitting there and saying, "that's crepitus, that's crepitus," because I'd learned about it. And it was crepitus, and he was desperately ill.

I remember being worried about speaking about his condition on the radio telephone because it was listened to by the people all along the Straits. You couldn't speak to the doctor privately, and I was very worried that the family of this man would hear that he had gangrene. I remembered enough Latin to put the condition into Latin, and the doctors understood. The families must have wondered what I was talking about, but that's what I did. Eventually this man recovered. I cleaned his wound all the time, and I don't quite remember the final outcome, but I think he did go out to a hospital in Quebec for surgery. But he lived.

There was another man in the same ward who was dreadfully ill. He had a bowel obstruction, and he had to be operated on. I did manage to get him out. I think an aircraft came for him.

However, most cases were straightforward. The time passed, and I must admit that I did get very tired, and I also had some kind of an eye infection. It wasn't serious, but it was a bit of a misery.

Doctor Hodd came back, and he settled down for

a while. He decided that I had to have some help. The next nursing station to Harrington was called Mutton Bay. I don't know if they ever had any sheep there, but it was called Mutton Bay. It was a bit further along the coast. There was an elderly nurse there named Miss Hewitt, and she had been there since time began. Everyone knew Miss Hewitt. So the message went to Miss Hewitt to come to Harrington to assist Nurse Fortescue and to come as soon as possible. Well, Miss Hewitt sent back many messages to say that she couldn't possibly come, as she had too many patients. Finally Doctor Thomas ordered her to come, and so she did.

She arrived by dog team, and towing along behind her on a komatik was a patient. She said, "I've brought an appendicitis with me. I couldn't leave him." Thankfully, Doctor Hodd was there. He was admitted, and we took out his appendix, and he was fine.

Miss Hewitt was very deaf, and she was a character. She said, "I can only stay as long as my batteries last, you know" (the batteries in her hearing aid). I said, "It's wonderful that you're here. If I do day duty, you can do night duty for a while." She said she couldn't do night duty, as she couldn't see in the night, and that she had better do days and I continue on nights.

Well, we managed for a while, but it didn't last very long. I think it lasted two or three weeks, and it was a great help. I don't know if her batteries ran out, but she finally returned to Mutton Bay.

Things went along, and every now and then I would get a message from Doctor Curtis, who was at St. Anthony and was Mission superintendent. The message would say, "Hold on, Fortescue. Help will be coming." Or, "Keep going, Fortescue. Nurse arriving soon." I suppose this was to keep me going.

Anyway, things went along, and we had Christmas there, I remember. Miss Dumont was not very much help, because she seemed to have some sort of breakdown and retired to her bedroom. She said she had done as much as she could do and that this was a terrible place and she'd had no idea that it was going to be so awful. She'd like to go home, but there was no way to leave and the next best thing was to just give up and stay in her room. I remember Miss Tucker and I used to take her meals and leave them outside her room. We hardly ever saw her.

Miss Tucker wasn't a great deal of help, and I told her she would have to leave the handicrafts once in a while and help me. She was very devout. She prayed a lot, and she endeavoured to be helpful. One incident, I remember. We had sterilizers for the little operating room, and they were strange contraptions. They had to be watched. There were many dials, and when the steam reached a certain level, you had to turn a certain knob. You mustn't let it go beyond another level, and eventually you hoped that everything inside had been sterilized. So I used to ask Miss Tucker if she would sit and watch the sterilizer, just to watch the dials so I could do something else. Miss Tucker wasn't very good at that either, and she often wandered off.

The spring came, and I was due to leave. I only had one long dog team trip, which was quite interesting. There was a very sick woman some distance away in a small community. I don't remember the name. The message came that the nurse must come, so it was decided—well, I suppose I decided—that I must go. I had never been on a komatik, and they really didn't tell me much about them. There was a driver, of course, and a team of dogs and this komatik. There was no komatik box on it, and I wasn't quite sure what I was meant to hold on to.

The hospital was at the top of a hill, which meant going down the hill at great speed. I got on the komatik, and I had my bag that I needed for nursing. He started off, and I came off bag and all. The driver went on down the hill, but he came back. I remember getting to this place after quite a long time. It seemed like an hour or two. Mostly it was straightforward going, but occasionally there were these little bushes, and I just remember it was not very comfortable.

We got to the house, and there were two men there. There was just one room and another room above, where you went up a ladder and there was an opening in the ceiling. The woman was up there. She was very ill, and I said she needed to go to the hospital. These two men—I think they were her brothers—they went outside and made a komatik box while we waited. The driver helped them, and they fashioned this long box attached to the komatik.

They brought her down. They had nothing in that house. It was stark and cold. They put in the rugs they had, and we laid her down in the box. I now stood behind, and I had something to hold on to, because I held on to the komatik box. And off we went.

We got back, and they carried her in. She had lost a baby, and she was infected and was in a bad way. But she never complained. No one ever complained. Never. They never complained of anything. Nowadays people would complain of the food or "too cold" or "too hot." There were no complaints. Anyway, she lived. I don't know how she lived, but she got better.

The time came for me to leave, but nobody else arrived, so I couldn't leave. These little messages came across the Straits, "Hold on, hold on!" Finally, two nurses did come. Doctor Hodd introduced them to me, and I took them 'round to the patients and packed up my things. I left on the same boat they came on. I left for Montreal. I remember I was all bundled up in parka and boots, winter gear, because that's how I had arrived.

We went up the St. Lawrence, and suddenly there was great commotion, because the ship had broken her rudder. There was still ice in the St. Lawrence, and she couldn't steer, I seem to remember. She weaved her way onto the drydock, and settled on to the drydock. It's quite an experience to be on the bottom of a drydock with your suitcases. I had to climb down the side of the ship on a rope ladder and up the stairs of the drydock, which seemed to be a mile high, on a wooden ladder. Somebody helped me, but I remember it as if it was yesterday, looking up at the top and thinking, *I can't get up there.* But of course I did, and there I was.

It was Lévis, in Quebec. I didn't have a great deal of money, and I didn't have any tickets or anything like that. There was a man standing at the top of that dock, and he was very nice and said, "Where are you going?" I said I was going to Montreal, and he said, "Would you like me to drive you to the station?" It sounded like paradise just to get in a car and drive somewhere! I said, "Oh, yes, thank you very much." So I got in this car with him, and he drove me to the station.

The arrangement was that I would arrive in Montreal, and my good friend Dorothy Davis, who was nursing near there, would meet me. It was hot there. It was springtime, and I was all bundled up in my furry parka. I remember Dorothy standing there in a nice dress and looking at me and saying, "My goodness, me! Where have you been?" After that, it was lovely. We had a holiday together on Lake of the Woods. It was just wonderful.

Then it was time for me to get back to North West River. I must have flown, I don't remember. I remember walking along the dock there at North West River, and Tony was walking in the opposite direction, and he passed me and walked right on. I stopped, and he stopped, and then he came back to me and said, "I didn't know you!" I was so thin, and I had blepharitis. My eyes were in an awful state, and I must have looked just dreadful, even though I'd had those two good weeks. He sort of said, "What has happened to you?" I said, "Well, that was Harrington." However, it was lovely to be back.

The plan was that I would fly back to England, and then I would come back and we would be married. I returned home, and I remember my father was then living in this house called High Standing that he'd bought during the war, on this big estate. Everyone said, "who is it you're marrying?" and, "Why isn't he coming over here?" I tried to explain that he couldn't think of coming to England to get married. He was very busy. I just had to get a few things, like a dress. Everyone wanted to know what this Tony was like. Strangely enough, my father wasn't in the slightest bit worried. All he said was, "I'm sure she knows what she's doing." I had a very elderly cousin, and he was extremely worried. He took me aside and said, "Are you sure that this is going to be all right?" I said, "this is what I want to do," and, "He's a very fine person. You'll meet him one day."

I think I stayed about three weeks. I remember I had to visit Tony's aunt and one cousin. They wanted to meet me, and it was more important than anything that I should meet them. So I drove down to Cheltenham where Aunt Jessie lived, to be kind of vetted, you know. Tony had said that he would be marrying this English girl, and she would be visiting. He had told me all about Aunt Jessie. So I drove down, and there was this big house with this long driveway, May Place, it was called. I stayed there two or three days, and it was just like going back in time. Aunt Jessie had house maids and parlour maids, and I had this big bedroom. After I had been shown to the room to wash my hands, as it were, I was shown to the drawing room, where I met Aunt Jessie.

She wanted to know all about me. "So you're going to marry dear Tony, are you?" I said "yes," and she said, "Where will you live?" I tried to explain. It's hard to explain to you young people how things were in those days, with *that* generation with *that* upbringing. She was an old lady. We talked and talked, and finally she said, "Fortescue, Fortescue. Are there other Fortescues in Essex? There was another Fortescue who married a Howard." Oh, good, I thought, because I went to school with a Howard. I said, "Well, I was at school with Jennifer Howard." She said, "Jennifer Howard. Well, let me see, now."

I said, "I remember her father was Thomas Howard." "Oh, Thomas Howard!" she said, "Oh, yes, Thomas and his wife So-and-so. Yes, that's right."

The Paddons are remotely intermarried with the Howards somehow, and that pleased her. You might think she was a dreadful snob, but she wasn't. She just liked to know families. Anyway, she was very kind to me and she gave me lots of mementos and wished me a very happy marriage.

The other little anecdote that might amuse was that Uncle Dick Paddon, who was in the navy during the war, always went to see Aunt Jessie when he was ashore. And they would greet him warmly and say, "You've been at sea, and you must need a drink." Dick thought it would be a nice whisky, but it was always lemonade. Dick used to tell that tale.

From Aunt Jessie's, I went into Cheltenham and bought a wedding dress, all in about half an hour, and went on to see Alouise in Bath. Alouise was a second cousin. She was a Van Summer, and there was some kind of misunderstanding between the Van Summers. There was Aunt Bessie and Aunt Annie, Uncle Willie, and Uncle James. One of them, I think it was Willie, went off to America and married an American. My dear! He married an American, Miss Van Tassel, and brought her back to England. There was some little problem. Anyway, they settled in Bath and had two daughters, Rachel and Alouise. They didn't get on very well with the rest of the family. Alouise never married. She lived in a big tall house in Bath. Rachel married a Captain Maitland. The two sisters had some frightful row and never saw one another even though they lived 'round the corner. Alouise was a "character," as they say. I knocked on her door, and she opened it, and I said, "I'm Sheila Fortescue." She said, "Oh, yes, yes, you're going to marry Tony! Oh, yes, come in." So I went in, and she said, "I've heard from Tony that you'd be coming, and he said 'give her some sherry to start off.'"

Alouise brought in a tray with two large glasses, and we each had a very large sherry. She was very funny and quite elderly. She lived in this large old house with this little dog and a very elderly maid. She said, "Don't do much cooking, but here it is, come on." We went into this vast dining room which would have held 40 people, and we had a meal and talked. She was fine, and she talked about family history and squabbles and so on. I left her and drove back to Essex, and I left soon after that. My sister Val was very worried about everything, and she said, "Do you have everything?" I said that I had a dress and something to put on my hair, and she said, "And shoes? White shoes?" I said I didn't have white shoes, but I went and bought some.

My father gave me six bottles of champagne, and I said goodbye to everyone. They all looked quite sad, and my father drove me to Heathrow. He didn't say much other than, "look after yourself," and, "Come and see us and bring Tony." I said we would come just as soon as possible. And we said goodbye.

In those days you could carry six bottles of champagne onto the airplane—anything you liked. I had a wedding cake in a box as well. So I flew back again, and somehow I got all this stuff to North West River, and there was Tony and his younger brother John to meet me.

MARRIAGE

Soon after I got back, it transpired that the nurse was leaving, and would I do the nursing again? I said yes, and when was the next nurse coming? They didn't really know. I got back in June and the idea was to get married. That finally happened in September.

I dug out my uniform and did the nursing and everything else. Occasionally Tony would send a message to Doctor Curtis about getting a nurse to North West River but didn't get a straight answer. The summer went by, and finally we decided that, nurse or no nurse, we would get married next Saturday, September 20, come what may.

Then Tony's brother Dick arrived with Lydia.

I remember the hospital was full, and we were very busy. It had got all 'round the community that we were going to be married on Saturday, and there were great preparations going on. Anyway, Saturday came, and I was in uniform at the hospital and I remember darting to the church to see if all was okay, and then darting back again. We did an operation, I think it was a hernia, in the morning.

We were to be married at six p.m., and Jack Watts was to give me away. I was working until about 4:30 and fairly busy, although I did have two aides. May Sooley—who became May Baikie—she was wonderful. She was going to help me get dressed and tidy me up and so on. And the other one was Mina Blake, who became Mina Hibbs. Mina and I went up to Jack Watts' house, and I got into this wedding dress. Jack was at the bottom of the stairs calling out the time and asking if I was ready and saying, "You shouldn't keep the doctor waiting, you know."

Finally I was ready and came down, and Jack and I as well as May and Mina walked the short distance to the church. Dick was the best man, and the church was very full. There were even people in the basement. Reverend Lester Burry was the minister. He had been there for years and years and was somewhat absent minded. However, all went well and little Margaret Paddon was a kind of bridesmaid. She walked along behind and then went and sat with her mother, Peggy.

We were duly married and came out and stood on the steps, and suddenly all the guns went off. I didn't know this was going to happen. *Bang, bang, bang, BANG!* Nobody had told me, and I just hung on to Tony. Together we walked down to the new dormitory building where there was to be the "time," the reception. But the dormitory was not finished, and the time was to be in the big room upstairs. There were no stairs, so they very kindly put this ladder up to this big window, and I gathered up my long white dress, and we all went up through the opening.

Everyone was there, although I didn't know a great many people. I had nursed some of them, but I wasn't sure of many names. There was a band playing with a fiddle player, I'm not sure who they were, but they wanted Tony to dance with me, and he absolutely refused. Which was a bit embarrassing. His mother was there shaking her head and saying he never would, and others were saying, "Oh, Doctor, you have to dance with her." But he wouldn't. Anyway, Sid Blake came up and he danced with me. It was wild! He swung me around off my feet and they played and they cheered and they sang. There was lots to eat, and it was quite amazing to me that they had done all this for us. Wonderful food and music and good cheer, and they were so kind, and it finally all came to an end.

I was to move into the Paddon house, obviously, so Tony's mother had rearranged things a bit and had put me in her room. Tony was still in his room, and she was in another room. Now later on Margaret Blake went into labour, and so we were very busy with her. She delivered in my old bedroom in the hospital.

The replacement nurse hadn't arrived but she did soon after, and I settled down to married life.

In those days, we had a generator in the basement of the house, and that provided power for our lights and so on. But after a short time, it was decided that we needed something better. Tony built a powerhouse outside and installed a very large—I think it was called a Lister diesel—and he also put in a small Kohler beside it, along with a battery of cells. This worked very well, most of the time. We also provided power for our neighbours, I think four different houses nearby. As I remember it, the lights were turned off for all of us at ten p.m. It was necessary to give warning that the lights were going to be turned off, and we did this by flashing them on and off several times, waiting a few minutes, and then turning off the generator.

When Tony was away, it was my responsibility to turn off the generator for the night, and this went well. There was just one occasion when I must have made some mistake, and apparently I de-polarized the power. I seem to remember a lot of sparks, and it was very alarming, but eventually it was reversed. I don't think any serious harm was done. On another occasion, after I'd turned off the power and was returning to the house on a very cold night, one of my boots came off in the snow, and I couldn't get it out. I was left with a small sock on one foot, and I was very alarmed, because I was worried about the children who were asleep inside, and I thought I might freeze one foot. However, I managed to get the boot out, and all was well. It wasn't a very satisfactory arrangement at all times.

The Grenfell Mission felt it was very important to be as self-sufficient as possible, because of course it was very difficult to get supplies in, in those days. Vegetable gardens were encouraged, and also some livestock. When I arrived in North West River, there were large vegetable gardens, and we grew enough root vegetables and cabbage and so on to supply the hospital and the dormitories and to send along the coast to the nursing stations. There was a very large greenhouse, very well sited and heated sometimes, and, of course, dependent on the heat of the sun in summertime. We started vegetables in that, and then they were transplanted outside.

Ellis Michelin was in charge of the gardens. He was very efficient and very hard working, and we depended on him a great deal. We also had a number of cows when I was there in the early years. We had six, and I think we must have bred them, because they were usually in milk. I don't remember a bull, but they calved, so there must have been one. They were characters. They all had names. They were milked in the morning, and then they were let out of the barn and they could wander at will, which they did. They would wander through the community and down the portage path to the beach and into our garden. You'd see them coming up from the beach and they'd push their way, quite often, through the clothes on the clothesline. It was said that sometimes they ate the clothes off the clothesline. Maybe it was just a rumour. I never saw that happen. However, they gave good milk, and we made butter, and we set the milk and skimmed it and made cream. It was an excellent arrangement.

We also had pigs. They were fattened and killed, and we had bacon. Altogether, in the essentials we were self-sufficient. The rest of the supplies came up by freight boat. It would come in the fall with the supplies for the winter, so we had to put in a requisition for what was needed to see us through to the following spring. This was done by the Mission, and it was quite an undertaking, I'm sure, because apart from the patients in the hospital, there was the staff and their families. I remember having to make out a list every Saturday for my supplies for a week.

We also had chickens, a great many chickens, so we had fresh eggs all the time. Apart from the Mission chickens, we had our own at the house. I had been involved in farming just before the war, and I was hoping to carry on with dairy farming. I had milked cows and ploughed and so on, but the one thing I could never do was look after the hens. Not at all. But we had hens, and they had to be fed and the eggs collected, and so, that was done.

Tony and I once did a Caesarean section on one of

the cows. The calf had died and had to be removed, so we did it one morning. Tony knew a great deal about anatomy, but he wasn't familiar with the anatomy of a cow. We found a very old veterinary surgery book of his father's printed in about 1890. It did give a diagram, so we propped that up on a corner of the barn, and I read it out to him while he proceeded, until I had to help him. We gave her an anaesthetic in a vein, and the book said to put her down on her left side, so we leaned against her until she gave way and gracefully toppled over onto her left side. We did the section. It wasn't very difficult, and then we sewed her up. After a while she opened her eyes—they have beautiful eyes, you know, with long eyelashes—and we helped her up. The next day, Tony had to leave on the hospital ship for his northern trip. He gave me instructions for what to do with the cow if there was any trouble, but she gave no trouble at all.

The next year, the same thing happened, and we had to do a repeat section. I think it was after that that we had instructions from Doctor Curtis at St. Anthony that we would no longer be keeping cows at North West River, and they were to be disposed of. They cost too much money, and now we'd had two C-sections, and it seemed to be the right time to go onto tinned milk. That was a great calamity, I thought.

Around about this time, the Grenfell Mission started to get some flying hours from the government. Before that, it had been dog team for years. This involved many, many weeks and was very difficult at times but was undertaken as a matter of course. So Tony was able to fly everywhere on the coast and could see a lot more patients in a shorter time, and it seemed to work very well, as I remember. But in the summer, the hospital ship, the Maraval, continued to make journeys on the coast with the doctor. Tony would often be gone for several weeks. People were very scattered on the coast, and he always visited every family, always.

One winter, Fred Rich at Butter and Snow was taken very ill suddenly, and his son Sandy came up by dog team to ask Tony to go down right away. Tony said yes, he would come, as soon as he could get ready. So he did, and he went out expecting the dog team to be there, but unfortunately Sandy had gone back to Butter and Snow without him. I remember Tony coming back in and saying that he would just have to walk. It was about four or five miles, and it was very cold.

He started off on snowshoes, and he walked some distance. Then he heard the airplane behind him. Every evening the pilot, Tommy Watt, who was a very experienced pilot and a great friend, would come in for coffee and a chat at nine p.m. So he dropped in as usual, but I told him that Tony was walking to Butter and Snow, so he went out and he got the airplane going and taxied (it was too dark to fly) until he found him and offered a lift. What a good man he was. So Tony got a lift to Butter and Snow and saw Fred and took care of him, and then Tommy gave Tony a lift back home. That's the sort of thing that happened now and then.

By 1955, we had absolutely outgrown the old hospital. There was no space left in it. I think it was built to take about six or eight patients, but there were 22. Some of them were in small cots for children or babies, but they were everywhere, and it was not possible to carry on. So in 1954 we started to build this new hospital behind the old one. It was quite a different construction from the old one altogether. It was a long, two-storey building, and it had wards and an operating room, a sterilizing room, an isolation room for infectious cases, and a babies' nursery. Also staff quarters in a wing in back and a very nice staff dining room and living room. Also a very fine kitchen on the ground floor. There was a lab and office space and everything that a small hospital needed. We were very fortunate to have it.

The nurse, who was Jean Smith and who had been there for years in the old hospital, was very reluctant to leave. She had been there for seven years when I came as a nurse, and when I got married, she came again. It was almost impossible to dislodge her. She just sat in her room and said she wasn't going to move and go over to the new place. No, no, not at all. Eventually she moved, but she didn't care for it very much.

Everyone worked on the new hospital. The Innu came over and worked, and people came in from other places, and we built it, and it was very fine. Of course we had to get rid of the old hospital, which was right in front of the new one, and it was decided to blow it up. Jack Watts decided that this was the best thing, and I think perhaps it was dynamite? But in the end we blew it up—all except for the chimney. It stood there for some time and eventually had to be pulled down.

Every so often, Tony had to attend meetings in New York when the International Grenfell Association directors met. Doctor Thomas would also attend, and they both had to deliver a report and discuss problems with the directors. In 1962, I was going to have a baby, and Tony decided that I should see someone and get a checkup. I felt fine, but he was worried, so it was decided that I would go to New York with him and see this doctor, and we would have a couple of days in New York.

We set off from North West River in the huge, old, navy blue International Grenfell Association snowmobile. There were seven or eight of us aboard, and I know Zack Tuttauk was there. From North West River up to Goose Bay, there was just a very narrow track. The snow wasn't cleared anywhere in those days, and you just drove along on top of the snow as best you could. We seemed to go along okay at first, but about a third of the way along, we broke down altogether. It was decided that everyone should walk on to Goose Bay, but I couldn't do that. So it was decided that Tony and I would start off walking, and the others would go on ahead. If they found someone with a snowmobile or some kind of vehicle, they would give them the message that we were behind and needed assistance.

Eventually someone came back and said that some distance ahead, there was a tent with someone in it. So we decided to go there and wait. We walked, and we walked, and it seemed like a long way, but eventually we did arrive at this tent. It was on the right hand side and fairly small, and I remember Tony saying that if a hot drink was offered, then I should take it.

There was one old gentleman in the tent. He had a fire in his stove, and he and Tony knew each other. He got his fire going and made some kind of hot drink, and I drank it. They both went to sleep. I found it pretty uncomfortable sitting up on the boughs, being about six months pregnant, but a few hours later someone came back for us. I guess it all got blown way out of proportion, because when help arrived, there were blankets and brandy and a doctor and, I think, a nurse. There was a tremendous fuss. However, eventually we got to Goose Bay, and we got to New York, and all was well.

I remember a time that Tony and I went camping, and we had a wonderful time. We had a pilot then, Geoff Henderson. He was quite an individual. He decided we should have a few days off by ourselves. He would fly us into a certain place, drop us off, and then return for us after a few days. I think we probably left on a Friday morning, and he would return Sunday afternoon to take us back, or perhaps Monday. This was very exciting, because we rarely got to go away together for something like that.

We packed a few things, and I remember he fixed a canoe under the aircraft, and he flew us to a lake that Tony knew of. I can't remember the name of it, but I can see it very well in my mind's eye. Geoff knew it well, and he dropped us there with all our supplies and then flew back. It was really quite incredible, because we were quite alone, just the two of us in Labrador, which hadn't happened before on a little vacation like that.

Tony was so pleased, and he knew just where to set up the tent. We had a tent stove, and the weather was good, and I think it was probably the first time that I had camped out in Labrador. I do remember all sorts of strange noises in the night, which seemed to be very close to the tent—scufflings and so forth—but nothing happened. The other thing I remember happening was this strange tapping noise coming from the shore. Tap, tap, tap, all night. It didn't sound menacing or anything like that, so I supposed it was all right.

It turned out that Tony had left his fishing rod in the canoe with the hook dangling over the side, and this unfortunate fish had been caught and was slapping against the side of the metal canoe repeatedly. It was a very eerie, very peculiar sound so close by. In the morning Tony told me that's what it was. But I remember the sound of it very well in the night.

PART II

LABRADOR DOCTOR, EXPANDED

Some of these stories come from outside the official records. Some are transcribed from documents in Tony Paddon's personal papers, while others are retold by me, based on my father's writings and additional documentary sources.

My father's autobiography always seemed to me to be incomplete. I think the book had to fit a certain format, and so much was omitted. My purpose here is to reveal the rest of it. There is more still, but I feel that his story is mostly told with the release of this book. I am sure his 10 months on North Atlantic convoy escorts would make a book on their own, but he just didn't write that much about them. Mostly he wrote about Labrador, and this was where his interests and passions lay.

The reader will note the imbalance between Tony's material and Sheila's. This is a simple reflection of how much was available. I don't know where he found the time, but my father wrote a great deal over and above what he had to write in his capacity as doctor and then Director of Northern Medicine. I can still hear his typewriter clacking away, and

I'm glad he found the time. Sheila never wrote much, and the recordings are really all the family has about her wartime and post-war life. I only wish she had *written more down. Every life becomes interesting as time goes by and society changes. I have become an inveterate nag to people about recording their parents, grandparents, aunts, uncles, etc.*

LABRADOR AS TONY PADDON KNEW IT

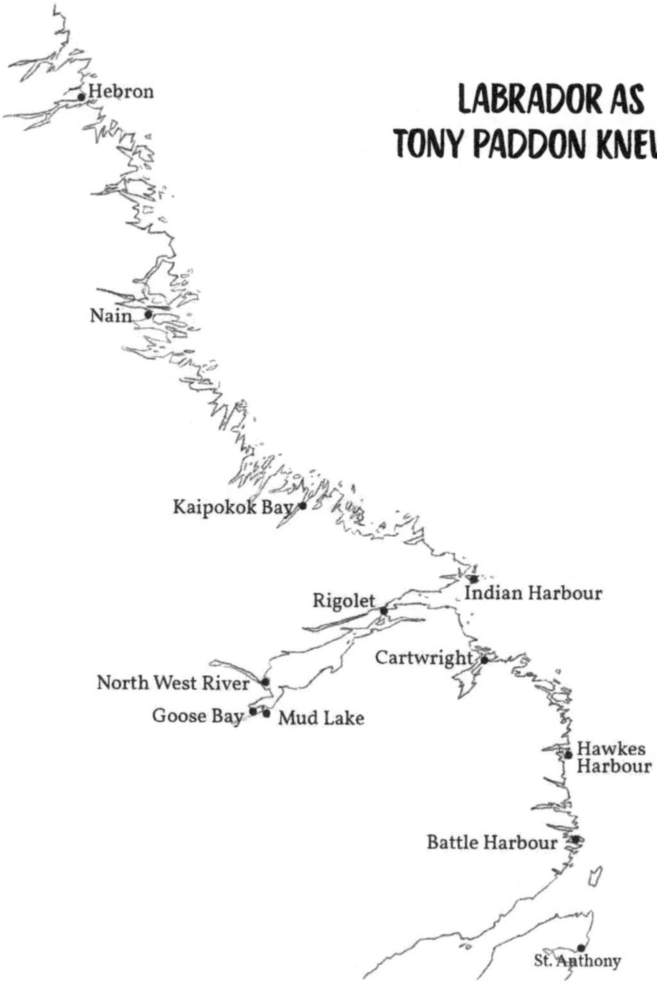

WARTIME LETTER

HMCS Kitchener
Care Fleet Mail Office St. John's
Newfoundland
August 1942

Dr. Claude Munger Director
St. Luke's Hospital
114th Street W.
New York City

Dear Dr. Munger:

Thank you very much for your last letter. Yes indeed, I shall count it an honour to provide St. Luke's with any properly censored little revelations about the intimate details of the British Navy. Just now I expect to be at sea for some time, so shall try to catch up with my correspondence. The typewriter has again folded up, but it will work after a fashion. Also, since I joined the service I find that I am forgetting how to spell. I hope you will be able to read this.

Shortly after I last heard from you we put to sea, bound for some famous Isles I cannot mention here. I might drop the subtle hint that they were once concerned with the management of what is now the United States but didn't make a very good job of it. I love them anyway and as a matter of fact I have at times wondered, after disinterestedly watching the new management, if the US might not be willing to go back to the pre-1776 status if given the opportunity.

The trip was full of the usual false alarms and whatnot, but nothing very exciting happened. We had a service passenger who learned the usual lesson about naval plumbing while depth charges were being dropped. With the explosion of a depth charge near the ship one may find one's self lifted three feet above the toilet on a solid jet of cold ocean, perhaps with jets of seawater spurting from both ears—truly the ultimate in enemas! Someone is always in the "heads" when we drop a pattern. Perhaps this lad was frightened when action-stations were sounded and had to go there. My first real break came when a brand-new English corvette sent us a signal that they had a patient on board with cellulitis of the leg. "Which is the corvette with the doctor on board?" they asked. We sent them a signal that the senior destroyer had a doctor on board. "Are you the corvette with the doctor on board?" she asked. "Two frigates in the group have doctors on board," we answered. "Are you the corvette with the doctor on board?" she asked patiently. "Yes," we capitulated. The captain did not feel much like stopping at the moment.

There was a heavy swell—there always is—and there was the usual excitement about the slipping gear, but finally our boat was released like something fired from a bazooka, and planed across the top of about three swells and partially buried herself in the fourth. I, as usual, got thoroughly wet. The swell was large, and the sea was very quiet, and in the troughs we would lose sight of the entire convoy for a while, and then climb dizzily and shakily to the top of a pellucid mountain and see them all heaving gently and reassuringly.

The other corvette was in the trough of the sea and rolling wildly. "Where the hell is your ladder?" with the grave courtesy of a Medical Officer just washed in the clean healthy Atlantic. "We lost it in the last port," they answered. "Come alongside and jump when she rolls." I was completely unenthusiastic. "What the hell do you think I'm in, the Fleet Air Arm?" was all I could say. As a matter of fact, landing on that thing was probably not unlike landing an aircraft on the average Merchant Carrier. Deciding when to jump was easy. If you jumped when you and the corvette were synchronous, you jumped straight up about thirty feet; if otherwise, you jumped across about fifteen. I am not in the commandos, so I chose the latter. After I took off, the corvette rolled the other way. Relative to the deck, I must have been travelling at somewhere near terminal velocity when I hit it, but fortunately there was an interested crowd of spectators about who broke most of the shock of the landing by not having time to get out of the way.

The patient turned out to have a large and exquisitely painful but thoroughly well matured abscess below his right knee. I gave him Pentothal Sodium IV and incised and packed it, and he felt better. Had lunch with them and held a clinic for the inevitable dozen or two other people who decide that they'd like to see the Medical Officer too. Found one pretty obvious (on history) peptic ulcer with probably slight bleeding, a nice fresh gonorrhea, and several minor complaints.

Time to return. Their captain explained, "My ship's first trip. Not really welded into an efficient ship yet. Very enthusiastic boys, but some of 'em are fresh out of training. Afraid we haven't much of a boat's crew yet. Would your captain mind terribly, do you think—"

I reflected that it was the stranger's turn to put out a boat, and that my own commanding officer might not be very grateful if I asked him to put out a second sea boat. "Delighted to do it, of course," the captain continued. "But I can't guarantee your personal safety, y'know. Frankly they're pretty green, what? Bloody deep, the bloody old sea. Up to you, though."

With a good deal of laryngeal spasm, I told him that I was sure that his boys, though lacking in polish, were quite competent, and I should be happy to accept his offer. Actually he looked pleased, perhaps because I had taken responsibility, which might exonerate him from a possible charge of manslaughter. The sea reeled wildly about us, and the ship rolled her rails down, and the boat's crew very obviously did lack 'polish,' even to the point of having to be shown where to sit. We had a big Scotch shepherd for a coxswain, and he did definitely know what he was about. Fortunately, he had a voice that stilled even the tumult of the sea. I made my peace with a Maker whom I had cruelly neglected for most of my life and waited. A vast shimmering blue-green sea rose many feet and reached for the sea-boat's keel. Gently she stirred. "Slip Slip Slip that Bleddy Dom gearrrr ye Lowland offal," bellowed the coxswain. There was a faint rattle of chain, and we glided silkily away on the breast of our liquid mountain. With your eyes closed, you would not have known we had left the corvette.

I looked at the coxswain. His eyes were bulging rapturously. "Did ye see, Sirr. Na bother ata. Meeraculous."

Kitchener, like all of her breed, rolls, and she was outdoing herself when we drew alongside. I will go on solemn oath to say that we had to fend ourselves out from under her rolling chock once to prevent her from sitting right on top of us and crushing us—as a tipsy hen might sit down too hard upon her egg and squash it. Our ladder was out, though, and it was easy to get onto it. She rolled the lower part of it under water after I was on it, but I was glad to get away without being submerged completely. I felt slightly weak, later, to observe the other corvette with her boat hanging vertically by its bows. They had had trouble picking it up after its return.

Lovely weather and lots of leave. I went down to Sussex on the south coast and spent a few days chopping down (and up) some extra trees on the grounds of a cousin. Left the south coast with a feeling that invasion cannot be very far away.

Fooled around in our ship again after that, killing time for the next job. One, very funny little episode. Had a nice practice shoot. It was at night, and the whole area was skipping with tracer and shells and God knows whatnot, and if I had been a passing ship, I should have stayed out of the way, with a number of ships firing guns and other and more secret things. One little coaster, apparently, got very mixed up. We were just turning for a run on a target and noticed a strange light almost on top of us.

"Who the hell is that?" quoth our captain. "Mr. Penney, illuminate him." Therewith, guns fired a star shell right over the light. There was a fiendish whistle from it—you may have heard star-shells—and I thought that whoever was under that light must have been a bit surprised. The star turned out to be a dud, so we fired another. Terrible crash and a whistle of shell, and by this time the light wasn't more than a hundred yards away, if that, and must have felt our gunblast right on his bridge. Then the whole thing was lit up suddenly by the star, and almost close enough to touch was this pathetic little freighter, drifting wildly, engines stopped. Even the ship was scared inarticulate, for her whistle was jetting silent clouds of steam, and her company were running around in circles. They apparently thought they were mixed up with an invasion fleet. They were just starting to abandon ship when we signalled them to clear out of a target area. I imagine their navigator was told a thing or three by their captain before the night was out. It sounds brutal, but we were all utterly helpless with laughter. The last time we saw him, he was travelling at what was probably four knots faster than his original speed trials, with a long curtain of tracer shells from another ship arcing high (and safely) over him.

Made a quaint little harbour later and sat there for a time very bored, with no shore leave. Our favourite destroyer was anchored next ship, and during my watch (anchor watch is always a bore) I sent her a signal. I'll have to give her a fictitious name. "Poor thirsty old *Algonquin*. See Ezekiel 19, verse 8." The reference, in case there is no Bible left at St. Luke's, reads approximately, "For alas! she is planted in the wilderness in a dry and thirsty place." I thought it rather clever. In about ten minutes their lamp winked and back came, "Thanks. Not poor, not old, but see Hebrews 10, verse 8. The reference was, "Jesus Christ, the same yesterday, today and forever."

We had a cocktail party shortly afterwards. On the Heysham Belfast Boat, some of us returning from leave met two US Army nurses, who, incidentally, know the St. Luke's unit very well. They were on leave, and we persuaded them to come to our boat and visit a very quaint old town and be entertained by the Navy. The party was on *Kitchener*, but had to break up for breakfast. We carried it on the next evening on the destroyer mentioned above. The two nurses seemed quite thrilled and got along well with the Navy and the other girls, all British. Second evening one of the nurses did herself a little too proud on the Navy's rum, a beverage not to be tampered with, and became a wee bit nauseated—worse than that ultimately—and since the captain was away, she was shown to his suite and advised to lie down for a few minutes. She recovered later and rejoined the frolic. The next day the captain returned, and later came into the wardroom with a U.S. nurse's forage cap in his hand. "Who the bloody hell were in my bed last night?" he asked ungrammatically. "Oh," replied one of my good friends on *Algonquin*, "that belongs to the girl that the Medical Officer off the *Kitchener* had on board last night." "Couldn't he have had her somewhere else," the captain muttered grumpily, and there I was, confronted with a situation which could only be described as hopeless. One doesn't even try to talk one's way out of a situation like that. I might just as well have been guilty and at least have had the compensation.

I seem to have become the unofficial poet laureate for the escort group, and my work is in demand.

Unfortunately, one effort was a highly irreverent one about our most important Admiral on the Western end of our run. He deserved every verse of it for prematurely crowing about U-boats, and it is funny in my view, but inevitably someone relayed it to him, and my fate hung in balance until he decided it was indeed funny and has been passing it around to his friends. My respect for him has increased, and but for his own sense of humour I might now be peeling potatoes for the Royal Canadian Air Force or Army or some such lesser Force.

The most successful one is the Barber Pole Song, our quite distinguished escort group being so named because of its group insignia, which is a narrow band painted around the funnel of each ship, of diagonal red and white stripes exactly like a narrow cross section of a barber pole. It is set to the Scottish air "Road to the Isles" and shows signs of taking on and becoming popular not only in our own group.

Recently, I published an article in the *Canadian Medical Journal* on a passage of eight minesweepers from Vancouver to Halifax via Panama. I was the medical officer of the group and made some interesting—to me—observations about the effects of heat, salt loss, shoreside ailments, etc. in the group, and the Navy liked it and asked my permission to submit it to the Canadian Medical Association. I have re-prints and shall send you one.

The above is an effort to portray to you that your former Sage of the Minturn Medical Service, and ex-Resident in Medicine, is trying to do something useful about the Hitler Episode, and also trying to enjoy himself a little between voyages. From what I learn in dribs and drabs of news, the St. Luke's Hospital Unit has set a high standard here in Britain and elsewhere and is very well regarded, and the two girls I mentioned seemed very full of praise for it.

This typewriter has just had what appeared to be a final demise, but has been tinkered back to life by processes I learned while I was on the Surgical Service at St. Luke's, though I don't think it is long for this world, and I will try to get off a few words more. Not long after I wrote the first part of this letter, we struck the final outburst of a hurricane which, after doing its thing further south, decided to invade the sub-arctic ocean. We had the usual overture, with a day or two of terrible weather and seas followed by a few hours of sunshine and confused but oily seas, and then the usual really horrible shellacking with a fair amount of mostly minor damage about the ship, and a most exciting night watch during the worst night. Before I left the bridge, the ship was rolling formidably, with the course putting us right in the trough and the convoy course making it impossible to ease the ship at all. I recorded rolls of over fifty-five degrees each way—try to imagine it—and holding on at all was difficult. Shortly after I got myself tied in bed, I was called down to care for an injured rating. He had crawled out of his hammock to join the relieving watch and shot right across the beam of the ship without hitting anything until he hit the juncture of deck-head and bulkhead on the other side, producing a neat I suppose transverse fracture of the left patella.

The splint I had was not very satisfactory, and he moved about in bed with the ship's motion so that it was necessary to put him in plaster. I had to get in bed with him to do it, and the result would have completely awed Doctor Mather Cleveland. It looked like the fossil of something that lived in a swamp, and halfway through it had to be reinforced with a great warty blob that gave it enough structural strength to permit his leg to slam against the bulkhead occasionally without breaking a second time. It was really majestic.

After we had been in port a short time this last time, we heard that Italy had just surrendered, and a few minutes later all ships were ordered to "produce tangible evidence of the Navy's satisfaction with this latest development," with the result that bunting was run up, the whistle and siren were tied down, and the mainbrace spliced on every ship in harbour ("negative ships at sea unfortunately") with a tremendous tot of the king's rum for every officer and man (over twenty) in all the ships. Those under twenty got "1/10 of a pint of lime juice appropriately sweetened." The single tot left my eyes swivelling and started a wardroom party that ended up many hours later on a beautiful new English destroyer that happened to be near us, when we put the last of their officers to bed and rolled home for breakfast wondering just what the hell difference the collapse of Italy really made anyway.

That seems to be about all for the time. I therefore wish you and anyone else interested in my attempts to carry on the St. Luke's standard here the very best and shall inform you of any further developments on the lunatic fringe of the sea war.

Best regards— [Tony Paddon]

FLY IN THE OINTMENT

There is no date associated with this letter, and it was, perhaps, a victim of wartime censorship. This is one of the few stories that Dad would tell us about his war experience. Nothing very disturbing and no deaths or injuries. I have sometimes wondered how long he would have had to live before he would tell us of some of the more brutal realities of war.

Events which otherwise might have been quite frightening sometimes seemed to invest themselves in a comforting cloak of broad farce. By way of example I recall one afternoon on an east-bound convoy when my corvette, *HMCS Kitchener K-225*, received a signal from the medical officer of *HMCS Kootenay* informing me that he had an apparent case of appendicitis, namely the captain's steward, and requesting that I come over to help. The medical officer, if I recall correctly, was one Charles Eliot. My commanding officer, Bill Evans (Lieutenant-Commander of the Royal Canadian Naval Volunteer Reserve) was to provide the whaler for transfer by seaboat, and this was accomplished faultlessly, despite a somewhat lumpy swell, and I soon joined Eliot. I agreed completely—it was most certainly a classic case—and we decided to operate at once. Penicillin was not to become available for another year, sulfonamides were unreliable, and as of August 1943, a rupture could have bad results for the steward. In these destroyers, the captain's cabin was designated a casualty centre, being a fine large room right across the width of the ship, complete with portable operating light and a good table. It was by now getting dark, and the sea was rising. The captain dropped by, was told the decision, and was asked by me if it would be possible, at the crucial moment when we were severing the appendix and then putting a purse string suture around the stump, to turn down wind for a short time, because this was the only part of the procedure where rolling would present problems. He suggested that the other steward call up the bridge by voice tube when it was time to steady the ship. The sick berth attendant was efficient, the surgical instruments were soon laid out neatly on the instrument tray, and the patient, sedated but nervous, was put to sleep with open ether (with a dash of Pentothal for encouragement), the abdomen was scrubbed, prepped, and then draped. We had a darkened room but a brilliantly lit operating table. Below us we heard the surge of *Kootenay*'s remaining oil fuel washing back and forth as we rolled, with only a bit of steel to separate us. If I remember correctly, I think I was the senior of the two surgeons by a few weeks. He was to open the abdomen, I to remove the offender within. He picked up the knife, and a large bluebottle fly suddenly appeared over the abdomen, flew a dizzy spiral and made a six point landing on the sterile field. A refugee, we were later told, from Gibraltar or some such place.

This was appalling. A single dirty fly foot-print

over the opened abdomen could potentially cause a fatal postoperative infection. We sprang into action with a couple of wet towels. At that moment the captain appeared at the door with a signal in his hands. The room, as I said, was almost dark, the unconscious patient lay in a pool of light, and two masked maniacs were dancing around in the gloom making wild swipes with towels into thin air. "What the hell are those two docs up to?" he said in a horrified voice.

"Oh" said the steward #2, "they are trying to kill a fly, Sir." "Christ—this is the last straw," said the commanding officer, as if this was the final act of two disintegrating minds. Luckily the fly returned to the abdomen and made a successful landing, being promptly squashed. While the steward went on to explain, the abdomen was painted with strong iodine, the new drapes applied, then we were again ready. The commanding officer told us that the westbound convoy only 30 or 40 miles to the north of us was under attack and *HMCS St. Croix* had been torpedoed and sunk. Most of her crew had been picked up by an English frigate, either *HMS Lagan* or *Itchen.* They were both sunk later, only three of *St. Croix*'s people surviving a second sinking, but I think it was *Lagan* which did the rescue and was next to be sunk. The commanding officer said that he couldn't therefore get too far out of station in case our own convoy was attacked, but would do his best when word came to run downwind ahead of the sea, which was still increasing. He asked what was the shortest time in which we could do the crucial work, and I guessed three minutes. The operation was effortless, and the appendix practically reared up on end to greet us. Word went to the bridge, and the next minute *Kootenay* was running smoothly and slowly before the sea, as steady as anything ever gets in the North Atlantic. Tying off the stump and burying it in the lining of the bowel was easily done in three minutes. Closure was no problem, and the patient awoke on schedule—his first words being wholly unprintable.

Later in the wardroom those off watch were discussing the misfortunes of the westbound convoy, which we gathered included the loss of four escorts and one or perhaps two merchantmen. There was no way to get back to *Kitchener*, so I slept in solitary grandeur in the captain's bunk. The next morning I was brought breakfast in bed, causing me a wild burst of alarm that I had been killed and was in heaven. I should have known that Eliot would not miss such a perfect chance. When I removed the napkin around what I took to be a glass of tinned orange juice, it was instead a small pickle jar, in which there was a neatly coiled appendix. Later that morning I returned to *Kitchener* by boat. Our convoy was not molested, but we now had a new worry, the GNAT or German Navy Acoustic Torpedo.

THE SCHOONER *CLUETT*

My father was notorious for not including dates in his writing, but I would guess that this was written in the early 1930s. He loved being on the water and could give very detailed descriptions of all the Grenfell vessels.

After completing my time at Lenox School I was to be a summer volunteer myself, and my brother Harry with me, both of us traveling to Labrador each June and serving in that capacity until early September. We travelled to Labrador and back on a recently acquired supply ship of the Grenfell Association, the very large schooner *George B. Cluett*, third of four supply ships bearing the name of the donor Cluett family, whose contributions to the Grenfell Mission were of great importance. Such cargo ships were vital to the far-flung Grenfell stations, and brought supplies from as far away as Portland, Maine. They were all large coaster vessels, the first three being auxiliary ships with both sail and diesel engines, the fourth being solely diesel propelled. The *George B.* herself was, before she was purchased and donated to the International Grenfell Association, a remarkable ship, being one of the largest two-masted schooners in existence, and almost an exact twin of another, the *I'm Alone*.

It is difficult to sort out the fact from the remarkable myths about the relationship of these two ships, but it was known that they were both built to be rum-runners during Prohibition. They made money carrying salt fish down to the West Indies and cargoes of rum back to the thirsty American coasts. Technically they could not be molested by the American Coast Guard patrols as long as they stayed outside the 12-mile limit, and they were unloaded to fast motor boats which then, under cover of darkness, fog, or foul weather, would ferry the cargo into the American shores, where there were trucks waiting for it. Fifty or a hundred tons of choice whisky, gin, and other drinkables always made a welcome treat for the thirsty American population, and a surprising amount of it reached their parched throats despite everything the Coast Guard could do. It was said that one of the two ships would bring back salt from Turks Island or some such Caribbean port, the other would bring liquor, and that they could turn into each other—being almost identical in any case—by various tricks. The one with the brown jib, the patched mainsail and the yellow dories was the *Giant King*, wasn't she? Her name plate even carried her name. Quite different from the *I'm Alone*—or did the *I'm Alone* perhaps also have a spare bunch of yellow dories and a set of *Giant King* name plates to exhibit when necessary? In fact it seems that these two ships may have worked together successfully for years, and repeatedly fooled the Coast Guard.

At last the *I'm Alone* was caught just outside the 12-mile limit—loaded with rum. The Coastguard cutter *Dexter* was determined to nail her this time, but she refused to stop for examination, being on the high seas, and fled at top speed. The *Dexter*'s captain got angrier and angrier, chasing along behind her and threatening to sink her if she didn't heave to for examination, and, hundreds of miles outside the 12-mile limit, the captain finally broke down entirely and warned *I'm Alone* to heave to at once or be sunk. Her captain wagered to his crew that the cutter wouldn't dare sink him out in mid-Atlantic, but lost his bet, for she was indeed sunk by gunfire, one man aboard drowning and the rest finally being rescued by their foe, half dead from exposure. Thus began an international "incident," the British Government angrily demanding to know why the Americans had sunk a British-registered ship far out in international waters. The case dragged on for years and is said to have made many lawyers prosperous, but it bankrupted the syndicate that had owned one or perhaps both ships, and the *Giant King* went up for sale, an ideal ship to replace the Grenfell Mission's previous supply vessel which had also got in trouble with the Brazilian government, though not over rum-running, and been permanently impounded over an extortionate salvage claim.

Giant King was acquired, given the new name of the *George B. Cluett,* and re-modeled to our needs. She was given two small but extremely heavy duty engines, and she was to last us until the end of the '30s. Each summer she left the USA, usually from Portland, Maine, with her hold and deck full of supplies such as food, grain, hay, cement, equipment and building supplies, medical supplies, and much else. She also supplied free transport for increasing numbers of our male volunteer staff. Accommodation was in temporary board bunks over the cargo. She would have flunked any health inspection, for she carried 40 boys as well as her crew, and the fo'c'sle would only accommodate 10 diners, so they were fed in shifts with no time to wash the dishes in between. The less said about the sanitary arrangements, the better.

Like all the large softwood schooners, her hull worked a good deal in any sea, and the ladder by which we entered and left the hold was always placed across the ship and would slide up and down the hatch coaming on which it rested as much as a foot or more as the hull changed shape when it rolled. The two engines gave her some six or seven knots, and she had a sail rig as well, although the huge main sail she had formerly sported was reduced to a small storm trysail to slow up her roll, but on her foremost she had an extraordinary variation, a huge square-sail on a 30-foot yardarm, a great help when the wind was right astern of her, and giving her another two knots speed. Correspondingly, when butting into a head sea she might well slow to a crawl or be stopped in her tracks, the two small engines unable to push her ahead. I have steered her for a four hour watch which started just abreast of the Liscombe Buoy outside the port of that name and found myself still just beside that buoy at the end of the watch. That fall the trip from St. Anthony to Portland took something like fifteen days instead of half that time, with head winds all the way.

She served a vital role, however, and carried everything we needed, distributing it up and down the length of northern Newfoundland and to isolated nursing stations and International Grenfell Association headquarters at St. Anthony as well as northward along the coast of Labrador as far as

North West River. Captain Iverson, a Lunenburger with a strong sense of humour and an inherited love of the open sea—and also a distrust of coastal waters—took her nonetheless through these uncertain waters year after year. He liked his young students greatly, and they him, and he could spin yarns of the rum-running trade in which he had done very well until the appearance of hordes of gangsters and hoods, at which time he chose to leave. Rum-running was regarded in Nova Scotia as a perfectly respectable business. From rum-running to working for a medical mission seemed to him a perfectly natural step, and indeed the modest respectability generated by working for Grenfell appealed to him. Mrs. Iverson was a long term president and member of the Women's Christian Temperance Union of Nova Scotia in their fight against rum, while the good captain was carting the stuff around the Caribbean and frequenting the American Coast, but both appeared to respect the other's point of view. Both were outstanding citizens in their community.

Kenny, as his friends knew him, was a born seaman, had seen everything including submarine warfare, and gladly taught his passengers to steer, handle cargo and generally learn as much seamanship as time permitted. Most of them left the ship in St. Anthony for distribution around the various stations until the return voyage in September, but some remained aboard for the summer acting as stevedores and freight handlers, and thought the world of the Nova Scotians aboard *Cluett*. Their good humoured and tolerant skipper had a permanent mate, a Mr. Byers, a large heavily bearded man who was said to shave annually with a blowtorch but was a consummate seaman. Chief Engineer Carmen Allen—wry, quirky, inclined to tipple in port, as a good sailor may, knew his engine like his own children. He was a short, thin man, but quick as a flash, and I saw him put our veteran Superintendent Doctor Charles Curtis firmly in his place in incandescent language when accused of something that was in no way his fault. In fact people who could put Doctor Curtis in his place were rare indeed, though he liked people to stand up to him, as I finally found out for myself, and he was filled with remorse if he felt he had done something unfair. Artie Cook, the cook aboard, was a very corpulent man, not very imaginative about his menus but able to produce good solid food when *Cluett* was standing on her head, turning out filling meals for the crew and the 40 hungry WOPs [without pays] very easily. As aboard most Nova Scotia schooners there was a lot of salt beef and fish, but splendid new bread, rolls, cakes, and muffins as well, and pies of all sorts. He liked to pose as a very stern, angry man but rarely fooled anyone long, and could play a zither and a mouth organ on a head piece, singing between times of lily white maidens, languishing lovers, and ghastly shipwrecks. His favourite was "Forget Me Not," rendered in a manner that would have melted the ship towing bollard. The life was spartan indeed, and doubtless they missed the good old rum-running days, but the crew were all neighbours and close friends at home, and wonderfully competent at sea.

Cluett thus provided transport back and forth for the volunteers (male only) and distributed the necessities to all mission stations. The trips along the coast in summer could be perfect, the autumn run south less so, for day after day the labouring hull would hurl itself into prevailing westerly winds and oncoming seas, and each time the massive thump would make the ship shudder. At times the propellers would race as they came out of water. The decks were never dry, the galley was noisome and dank, and since there was no heat anywhere except in the galley forward, it was impossible to get warm. The Nova Scotians had the gift of simply waiting patiently for better times, but my own love of the sea would run dry, and I would wish myself in the Sahara Desert. In the winter the International Grenfell Association chartered ship and crew to carry salt fish to the Caribbean, bringing salt back home. In addition, Iverson served as the International Grenfell Association's agent, purchasing on our behalf, meeting odd requests like one for a Holstein bull, a certain type of operating table, a few cases of tinned lobster, a thousand square feet of maple flooring—just about anything we could think of. She was disposed of in—I think—1939, later foundering off Scatarie Island in a gale of wind and heavily overloaded with coal. Those softwood ships worked, and if they worked their seams open, that was the end.

LOG OF *MARAVAL*, 1946

PART 1

Summer is over, and the ship is lying stormbound at Cape Harrison, Labrador. Soon we shall leave here, running North to Makkovik and Hopedale for the last trip of the season. Yesterday we fled north from Holton with a blustering southeaster behind us, and came rolling and staggering around the gloomy bulk of Cape Harrison to anchor gratefully in the restless waters of Webeck's Harbour. *Maraval* rolled wretchedly at her anchor all night, and the wind moaned dismally in her rigging. This morning dawned grey and lonely with heavy seas pounding the island at the harbour mouth. We could see the spray being driven right over the end of the barren spur and the sound of the sea came hollowly even to our anchorage. All day we wallowed miserably, but tonight the weight is gone from the wind. The seas still burst against the harbour mouth, but tomorrow we shall leave at dawn. No one is anxious to linger in this bleak apology for a harbour. Tonight seems a good time to begin the chronicle of the ship's travels, for no patients have come off today, and the two other ships in port have kept to themselves. Their tall spars can be seen, as I write, swaying against a lowering sky, but their decks have been deserted most of the day. Night is coming over the Cape.

Maraval came off dry dock late in May. The harbour at St. Anthony was technically open somewhat earlier, but the winter's packed snow and ice had to be shipped out from under her berth, where the hot spring sun could not reach it, before her cradle could be slid into the harbour. It was the end of the month before she was ready to sail, and she left almost immediately for Forteau, near the border between the Newfoundland and Canadian parts of Labrador. She reached that place after a day's steam, and there met Doctor Curtis, who had gone thither in *Cluett* with men and material to start the new nursing station which must now be just about ready to open. Materials were delivered by *Cluett* and work started immediately. Doctor Curtis then took *Maraval* south to confer with Doctor Hewitt at Harrington. I cannot report much of that trip, except that I recall the enthusiasm of Doctor Curtis upon his return. The beautiful wooded bays and islands of much of the coast between Bradore and Harrington, and most especially around St. Augustine, had quite captured his fancy. From Blanc Sablon and Forteau he reported quite a busy little clinic, and when the ship returned she had over a hundred names in the patients' register. Several of the more acutely ill were brought in by *Maraval* or their passages arranged on the mail steamer. One desperately ill boy had been brought aboard dying, and despite every measure succumbed to empyema.

I can speak more fully of the ship's subsequent movements, for I spent most of the summer aboard. On June 17, we left St. Anthony for Forteau, planning to do a fairly complete medical coverage of the southern Labrador coast from Bradore to Battle Harbour.

It was hoped that the trip could be more complete than usual, as staff and material shortages during the war had necessarily somewhat curtailed the ship's activities. The dispensary had been somewhat altered and improved, and the equipment aboard was as complete as ingenuity could make it in a ship of that size. The ship's X-ray, so sorely needed in this country, had not yet arrived, but all other equipment was complete and very satisfactory.

It might be interesting, at this time, to introduce the members of the crew. The captain is Captain Stanley Barbour, well known to seafaring Newfoundland. He has been master of every sort and size of ship sailing out of the country, and a veteran of the sealing steamers and the fishing fleets. He is a recognized authority on ice and on the special navigation problems relating thereto, which was to prove of great service to us later in the summer, and on the cod fishery in its every aspect. Never a port we entered but there were captains aboard to talk over the fishery and to hear his opinions on its prospects. His memory for the details of the fishery always struck me as remarkable, and he could give a detailed report of almost every catch along our itinerary to those whom it concerned. Some of the ships he has commanded could almost take *Maraval* aboard, but he seems to enjoy the little ship and to have a warm personal friendship for her. His knowledge of the whole coast is encyclopaedic, and he would cheerfully take the ship anywhere and at any time. He presides over his crew with the mildest of yokes, and a penchant for practical joking and skylarking seems to blend quite naturally with his dignity of office.

The engineer is Jim Styles, and almost anyone who has been long associated with the Mission will recall his father Will, of the *Strathcona.*" Will never viewed the diesel engine as anything but a noisy, smelly, unreliable upstart. When our last steam vessel, the *Strathcona*, was retired from service and sold, Will's heart was completely broken. Today he shovels coal in the hospital boiler room at St. Anthony, and at night when the old man occasionally nods in the glow of his furnaces there is a grin on the weather-beaten face which I can only interpret as signifying that he is again afloat with Sir Wilfred and firing *Strathcona*'s ancient boilers with good Sydney slack. Jim, nonetheless and to the old man's disgust, is a good dieselman. He nurses *Maraval*'s rickety old Fairbanks-Morse with the same affection his father lavished aboard our steamers, and cheerfully tries to forestall the inevitable hour when it will run no more. Plans are afoot for a new engine—please note, any reader who happens to have a nice, new heavy duty diesel he doesn't want—and Jim may then have the luxury of an engine upon which he can depend. For the meantime he continues to keep the engine going long past its proper lifespan, and the ship usually seems to leave port or arrive pretty well on schedule.

Absalom Colborne was deckhand, cheerful and brisk. Like myself he is a veteran of the White Ensign and was in the Royal Navy for most of the war. He and Ted Patey, the junior engineer, share most of the steamship together, and Ab should qualify as a good teacher. Harvey Wotton, the cook, made up the complete circle. The cook has the hardest job aboard a small ship, for Harvey, in addition to endless meals, myriads of dishes to wash, and the steward's work for the ship, helps weighing anchor, helps watering ship, helps washing down, and then must help bring his own wood and coal and supplies aboard. It would be interesting to know if anything could ruffle the cheerful aplomb with which he has attacked his job.

My medical assistant was Tom Eckfeldt, US Naval veteran and now a medical student in Philadelphia. A fast worker, he was most useful, and he began his surgical career, I believe, in my dispensary. He learnt to pull teeth with the utmost dispatch and accuracy, and left a trail of them in the ship's wake.

We left St. Anthony one gray morning, and picked our way across the Straits of Belle Isle. There was a long swell and a chilly breeze and a hint of weather to come. The Straits were foggy but not inordinately uncomfortable otherwise, although the dinner table showed at least one vacancy. Captain Barbour picked up the fog-shrouded shore north of Cape Amour, and we groped along the rocks and across the bay to Forteau. A very large grounded iceberg, which he recognized from the week before, made a useful landmark.

Forteau was a hive of activity, and the foundations of the new nursing station were already in. I was shown over the old building and recall that there were believed to be 28 recorded leaks in the roof. Men and materials were unobtainable during the war, and the old building has had to serve until this year. The nurse who inhabited that flimsy hovel during the war winters should have had a George Cross, and my respect for Miss Hewitt can hardly be overstated. It will certainly be a change to live in a warm, comfortable building and to have some good facilities to work with.

At Forteau there was one seriously ill child who responded well to treatment. Some minor surgery completed the picture, and we proceeded across the Straits of Belle Isle to Flowers Cove. This is a very busy nursing station with a large local population. It is in the efficient hands of Miss Jean Smith, and she called in as many as possible of the local people needing medical care. Bad weather prevented some of these in the outports from getting into Flowers Cove—it had blown a blustery western wind there for over a week—but in a day there, we saw 54 patients of various sorts. Several were referred to hospital. One baby was admitted in a state of complete starvation and, despite every effort, died the same day. The poor little creature looked like a Belsen Baby, and at seven months weighed but six pounds. Lack of proper food and lack of knowledge had contributed equally to its death. Were it not for Miss Smith, there would have been others this spring in the district.

It was pleasant to meet Ray Boyd, leader of the local co-operative movement. Ray has worked with patience and skill—and no little tact—to raise the living standards by education. I feel that much has been accomplished. Many goods can be obtained much more cheaply, and products can be marketed much more profitably in this way, but as Ray and his colleague Ike Newell at St. Anthony point out, it is the social education and the spirit of cooperation which has the more enduring and important effect. The old system of economic feudalism, of debt, dole, disease, and death, has been challenged by men like Newell and Boyd, and the results in Flowers Cove district, for example, are already palpable.

Flowers Cove hospitality included a magnificent lobster dinner, and Miss Smith is almost as good a cook as she is a nurse. Tom had extracted about thirty teeth, among other things, and was probably suffering from the stiff right wrist that seems to be an occupational hazard in this branch of the work. When I told him that, during a winter dog-team trip to Flowers Cove I had extracted three hundred teeth in three days, he looked impressed. I was bound to admit that such a hideous tally was exceptional, and that over twenty a day was a good average. For the benefit of the technically minded, all dental extractions are under local anaesthesia, and we are proud of the ship's reputation for good dentistry.

From Flowers Cove we recrossed the Straits to Blanc Sablon in Canadian Labrador. The first evening was a busy one, and at two o'clock that morning I was summoned out of night by two men from Bradore, 15 miles or so to the south, to see a woman who was described as "wonderful sick." She was, too, with bronchopneumonia and pleurisy, and in acute pain. Sulfathiazole and penicillin were administered generously, the pain was treated vigorously, and she was left asleep for the first time in two nights. I got back to Blanc Sablon in time for breakfast aboard. Tom had not been called during the night, as only one doctor was needed, and I did not wish to leave the ship unguarded.

We ran over to Bradore, in *Maraval* this time, and it was an improvement over an open motor boat on a frosty spring night. The patient was doing admirably, and we proceeded to cover the rest of the "town," including the French Canadian fishermen who had come in to meet us from the large community of Long Point nearby. There is no anchorage there for *Maraval.* My halting French did not prove necessary, and most of them spoke excellent English.

Upon returning to Blanc Sablon we finished up the work in that community and set our course for L'Anse au Clair, once more in Newfoundland territory. It was rough in this rather indifferent harbour, and we worked ashore in the home of a man named Thomas. His son, aged eight or ten, had a badly infected knee, and he was given ether and the abscess was opened and packed. Late in the afternoon we weighed anchor for Forteau, which was reached before dark. The ship had now seen over 160 patients, done a dozen minor surgical procedures, extracted one hundred and sixty teeth and fitted six pairs of eyeglasses. She had been at work five days.

Thereafter came a succession of places which I had never before visited. Curious names they were, and many of them are the relics of the first French fishing fleets on these coasts. The names have altered through several centuries. L'Anse au Loup is Lancey Loo, L'Anse au Diable is of course Lancey Jobble, and others have changed similarly. East and West St. Modeste, Fry's Cove, Barge Bay, Wreck Bay, Green Bay, Pleasure Island, Red Bay, and others came and went. Fry's Cove was the veriest crevice in the forbidding cliffs, so tiny that we went in astern and put out a line ashore over the stern in addition to our anchor to prevent swinging onto the rocks. Some of these places are seldom or never visited, and although great liners pass close by on their way through the Straits, their passengers can never know of the tiny hamlets and their battle against the cold and the fog and the ice and the uncertainties of the fishery and the ever-present hunger and disease.

The fish-cake that graces your breakfast plate may come at its source from just such a hamlet, and other hands went into its preparation than those of your cook—if you are lucky enough to have one nowadays—hands numbed with the cold and galled with saltwater and too often weakened by hunger. It is sad that the recompense for that labour is so small. It is not a very civilized world, really. We have only to consult our newspapers, of course, to suspect as much. It is this realization, conscious or otherwise, that makes us, in the last analysis, support such organizations as this Mission. There is so much to be done, and neither the time nor the resources to really do it. Often, in these desolate little communities, one thinks of hundreds of unknown little donors to our organization. What would you think, could you see how your money was spent? Some of you might have a sense of smugness and virtue. Perhaps that is inevitable. Could you, instead, have a sense of fellowship with these and with all men, then the Mission is doing its work the better for that. It should work two ways, this Mission of ours, to be wholly successful—both for those it serves and for those who make the service possible.

Red Bay was the next large community, and there we found a busy clinic. It was curious how many eye cases we saw in this village. The wear and tear on the eyeglass department was considerable, but I think good was done.

Anchored as we were right in harbour, one would hardly have suspected that the place would be a good fishing site, but Captain Barbour, who knows more about ways of the codfish than that creature itself knows, suggested dropping a line. Tom refused to believe that the great, crude unbaited hook could attract even a codfish, but was soon pulling them in almost as fast as he could work. There must have been a couple of hundred pounds flapping on the wet planking in half an hour, and the scuppers ran red when the cook began to split some for the ship's use. The rest were donated to a little boy who had come aboard as a sightseer, and he rowed away as pleased as punch. He could "make" these fish himself, and they would represent several dollars in real cash, a commodity that one suspected his family would find useful. The fish stopped as abruptly as they had begun, and for all I know have not visited that harbour bottom since. Tom and I reverted to pulling teeth.

We were away early, and the work continued. The latter part of the day saw us groping in heavy fog, with a nasty lump of sea. We tried repeatedly to work our way into Henley Harbour but found a strange maze of icebergs and salmon traps blocking the way. A slight lifting of the fog finally permitted us to edge into this excellent harbour, where we found the usual busy clinic. It was late when we were able to gather in *Maraval*'s galley for a cup of coffee and a comparison of notes, and although I found the inevitable leak in the deck over my bunk had, as usual, selected the head end of the bunk for its attentions, I slept deeply. I heard the staccato hammering of the generator engine as the anchor came in at daybreak, but turned over and slept late—disgracefully late. We had an uninterrupted run of many miles to Pleasure Island, a summer fishing station. The name was perhaps a euphemism, for we found a man with a gastric haemorrhage here and another of the same crew also urgently needed hospitalization. Both were put to bed aboard, and we ran on to Cape Charles, where an old friend, one-time housemother in the Grenfell School at North West River, was seen aboard and joined the ranks of our floating hospital with renal tuberculosis. Sad to say, she died not long after reaching St. Anthony. Both of the other patients, I hear, have prospered. At Battle Harbour a cancer of the throat was discovered—too late, alas, but a good number of other patients were seen. A little girl of seven acquired a glittering new plaster cast and was so delighted with it that one gathered she would have sacrificed the other arm too, had we been content to complete the set.

From Battle Harbour we went to our last port of call, Mary's River. It was surprising how little medical work I found, in general, in the Battle Harbour area. The reason was to be found at Mary's River, in the person of the indomitable Miss Jupp. She seemed to have done almost everything to be done in the area and had completed a most difficult job the night before our arrival, with the result that the lives of both mother and child had unquestionably been saved. I wondered at the time how I myself should have dealt with so difficult a situation, but did not quite have the courage to say that I should have been completely at a loss. A bronchopneumonia case was taken aboard and we sailed at dawn for St. Anthony, across the Straits.

The first trip was over, and several days of outfitting and replenishments would be necessary before the long trip of the summer would begin, a trip that would take us a weary distance and would see us locked in the ice, and would see us in difficult and trying waters. It was to be a truly useful and a most interesting one, too, and I said good-bye to Tom Eckfeldt at St. Anthony with real regret for his enthusiasm and ability. His successor, Bill Lawler,of Toronto, joined the ship the day after our arrival, which even almost coincided with the second arrival of *Cluett* from North Sydney with staff and cargo. We were met on the wharf by Doctor Curtis, who seemed well pleased with the results of the trip. Many new harbours had been visited, and there were four hundred-odd names in the patients' register. Our patients were driven up to the hospital and *Maraval* lay quiet by her large sister, the *Cluett*.

It is growing late, and this narrative must be dropped for a time. The ship rolls sullenly, but the wind has nearly dropped out. There are northern lights flickering over Cape Harrison, and the air is frosty. The melancholy roar from the harbour mouth subsides slowly, although there will still be a lump of a swell at sea tomorrow, and all must be secured in the dispensary against our sailing at daybreak when the *Kyle* is expected southbound with fishermen and mail.

PART II

The season has changed since I wrote the first instalment of this account of *Maraval*'s summer voyages. Just the other day, Christmas to be exact, I crossed lower Hamilton Inlet by dog team. Here *Maraval* had passed in September, past the rough and darkly wooded hills, then gay with the autumn gold of birches and the flame of berry bushes amongst dark spruce. Dark water had coiled smoothly along *Maraval*'s sides and stretched white and straight behind her, but now there was no water at all, but miles of tumbled sea ice and hummocks, and the hills had changed to pale undulations of violet and white in the silent distance.

It was on the third of July that we left St. Anthony bound north for the long Labrador run. Bill Lawler of Toronto had taken the place of Tom Eckfeldt as my medical assistant, and Miss Seabrook of the London office had joined the ship's company to make a first hand report of our work to the British branch. Otherwise the crew was unchanged, and we had already found the crew a cheery and efficient one.

We ran across the Straits of Belle Isle and spent the night at Mary's River, where Miss Dorothy Jupp's clinic was again reviewed. As usual the patients and the hospital seemed to be prospering under Miss Jupp's efficient reign, and we sailed at daybreak for Fox Harbour, where a young man with a bone infection of the leg was awaiting us. After a brief stop, we ran on into the long and almost land-locked port of Petty Harbour. It was a lovely morning to start something, or anything, crisp and bright and with a brisk west wind. Miss Seabrook and I could count over 30 good sized icebergs at one time. Outside of us schooners drove north under a good press of canvas, bound north for the summer's fishing. The sea was lively with marine life, and the captain's shotgun appeared on deck—object, duck dinner—and started a brisk controversy about game laws, and what constituted a migratory bird.

Spear Harbour, Murray Harbour, Francis Harbour Bight, and Georges Cove dropped after a brief visit in each. At Georges Cove the Mission used to operate a small summer school, until wartime shortage of staff curtailed it. It is hoped that we can reopen now, and I found the building well cared for and the people anxious to know when the teacher would be back.

At Fishing Ship's Harbour, Mr. Louis Dawe kindly gave us the facilities of his dock and sent down the gift of an enormous fresh salmon. Upon learning that we hoped to go up the long inlet to Port Hope Simpson, he very kindly offered us the services of his best pilot, as neither the captain nor I had been up the run.

The run up the narrow fjord to Hope Simpson is a beautiful one, and we had a sunny day. As soon as the sea was a few miles behind us, the mercury went up rapidly. Deer flies and mosquitoes came from miles around and hung above us, watching their chances. The rolling hills were heavily wooded, but I thought that the shores and hill tops looked rocky and lacked the promise of either Sandwich Bay or Hamilton Inlet. As we drew near the head of the inlet, the water became heavily stained with peat drainage and wood bark, and finally the buildings of Hope Simpson came into view. Great floating fields of peeled fir or spruce logs lay in the mahogany-coloured water, and a large English steamer drowsed in the sun, while a stream of logs flowed up her side and into the holds. She was loading pit props for the English coal miners.

Hardly had we anchored when the Labrador Development Company's nurse came alongside in a motor boat. There was a very sick man aboard the steamer. Could we see him? We did, and found that

Mohammed Ali (something unpronounceable) was the ship's donkeyman, a Moslem Indian, and that he was very uncomfortable indeed. Penicillin and other things appeared, and he was soon feeling rather better. He had, incidentally, been torpedoed a number of times, and we learned that he and I shared the same convoy on several occasions.

Miss Butler, the Company Nurse, seemed glad to see a doctor again and mustered her clinic aboard *Maraval*. Teeth flew in bloody streams through the dispensary door, and a haze of anaesthesia fumes gathered over the ship. Time out for a brief lunch was a mark of deference to our guest only, and we were able to finish the work in Hope Simpson by mid-afternoon. After saying good-bye to Miss Butler, we dropped down the tranquil bay in time to reach Williams Harbour before dark. It was some time before we were able to find water shallow enough to anchor in this rather peculiar harbour, but once moored for the night, the usual invasion by patients began and continued until late. One of them was a child apparently suffering from a post-diphtheria paralysis of the throat, and as if to confirm it the next patient, a young man, showed all the signs of full-blown diphtheria. We gave him a large dose of anti-toxin and some good advice, but there was little else we could do, and I had no wish to convert poor little *Maraval* into a pest-house. We heard later that he had made an uneventful recovery.

During the next days the ports went by one by one. Francis Harbour beautiful, Occasional Harbour neat, thrifty little Triangle Harbour, and the appropriately named Snug Harbour went by, each with its busy little clinic. At Venison Islands, patients crowded our decks almost all one day, and we picked up a case here for transportation to Cartwright for surgery.

The busier ports make lively times for the doctors. Generally speaking, it is best to eat and sleep in between ports while at sea, and to work steadily while in harbour until the work is done, so that the ship can get under way again. Visiting over 90 ports, as we did, it is necessary to set a fairly fast pace in order to get the work done. Bill and I worked together, one of us doing the dental work and laboratory work and taking calls ashore as necessary, the other one doing medical histories and examinations and also the minor surgery, eye tests, etc. The dispensary is small but very well compact, and it is surprising how much work may be done in so small a space.

The work is simple in nature, and consists chiefly of an out-patient clinic. There are a good deal of medical examinations, many minor surgical procedures, and some ante-natal examinations. Cases needing hospitalization are diagnosed and taken aboard for transportation to the appropriate centre, or their passage is arranged by the government mailboat, which transports many cases for us "on pass." Tuberculosis in all its forms is constantly watched for, as are such deficiency diseases as beriberi, scurvy, rickets, and the like. The settlers of the country and the floating population of Newfoundland fishermen who come North for the summer fisheries are the two largest groups seen, although there are a good number of Eskimos in the Northern part of the country and usually small bands of Indians at some of the trading posts.

Most of our patients are seen on board, but there

is usually at least one call ashore in most ports. One of us usually stays aboard to keep the clinic going, and the other climbs down into whatever dory, motorboat, or other craft has been provided and proceeds ashore or to another ship.

For several years it has been impossible to get dentists or specialists on the coast, and so we must fit a good many spectacles, usually by the simple subjective methods satisfactory for certain uncomplicated eye disorders, and always there are teeth to be extracted. Extractions under local anaesthesia are done by the hundreds. Next summer we hope to add to the ship's equipment a mobile X-ray plant, and thus learn more about tuberculosis in Labrador than has ever been known before. Without X-ray, all too many cases are missed, and too many people make long and expensive trips to St. Anthony or Cartwright only to learn that they need never have come or far worse, that they came too late to be saved. All in all the work requires a good deal of patience and a genuine fondness for the sea. Immunity to seasickness is almost essential. The work, however, has many compensations in its interest and in the results achieved. One likes it or one does not, and I am fortunate in enjoying it, for it is the most economical and indeed the only way to see most of the people of Labrador, where the population is remotely scattered, and we coordinate well with the other mission establishments, whose beds we help fill with the patients we encounter on our rounds.

Hawkes Harbour, of fragrant memory, is the site of Labrador's only whaling factory and quite an olfactory shock to the visitor. The manager of the whaling factory greeted us courteously and sent us a present of whale beef, which is excellent. We saw a number of patients, including a score of more of the factory hands. We were not, however, able to leave that night. *Maraval*'s elderly engine had been giving increasingly shaky service, and it finally packed up. Jim Styles began to develop the haggard look and wrinkled brow peculiar to ship's engineers with trouble. The next morning *Maraval* limped out of the harbour seeking a less perfumed atmosphere than that of a whaling factory in hot weather. It was Sunday, and we had been up the previous night working on the engine.

Squasho Run is a long cleft in the rocks and so narrow and regular in places that it might be an artificial canal. It separates Hawkes Island from the mainland. For miles a ship runs in the sound of her own wash breaking along the shore on either side of her. Down the corridor hobbled *Maraval*, and into a place called Boulter's Rock. Then to Comfort Bight, where my good friend Mr. Don Andrews runs a herring factory. The Mission has few better friends on the coast. At Frenchman's Island everyone seemed well, but at Seal Island there was no sabbath rest for us, but a very large and busy clinic. Thence *Maraval* steamed slowly and uncertainly to Weber's Harbour, where we were compelled to anchor. Little *Maraval* is as good a ship as she ever was, but the old engine is worn out with 17 years of hard use, and we were almost afraid to take it apart, for fear of what we might see. Bill went ashore to see patients, and then on foot to a nearby place, Corbett's Cove, to see a sick boy. I joined the engine room staff again in the engine room for another all-night session. Under Jim's supervision the engine was pulled down and checked over and finally, after he had been nearly 33 hours without a break, the trouble was remedied and we were able to continue. Needless to say, I was grateful to my crew. We have no union hours and no 40-hour week on board *Maraval*. There is too much to do. The crew knew that if the ship was urgently needed, and that if she were towed home, helpless hundreds of people would be deprived of their only medical care. They kept on the job with dogged faith until she was fit for sea.

No one thanked them or praised them. We sailed at once. Praise was unnecessary. They are men I can depend upon, and I am fortunate indeed. It is hard to ask them to take that engine to sea another year. It is hard to order the ship to sea with patients, women and children aboard in the autumn gales. If somebody wanted to make a gift to the Mission, I should think a new engine for *Maraval* would be about as welcome as most. It would to me. This is not a yachting country, and sometimes I worry.

With the tired old engine pinned together for a little while longer, *Maraval* pushed her bow into Batteau Harbour. Here there was a baby very ill with pneumonia. Transporting it was out of the question, so we gave it an extra-heroic dose of penicillin and went back to clinic. Several hours later, as we were leaving, Bill went ashore to give it another one. The *Reader's Digest*, he reported, was right about penicillin. The baby was almost normal again.

At Salmon Bight health was at a low ebb, and there was much to occupy us. Here, too, we picked up another patient for operation at Cartwright. Black Tickle, Spotted Islands (a one-time nursing station which it is hoped we can now reopen), Domino, Red

Banks, Wolf Islands, and Gready were visited. At this latter place, a bit of minor surgery removed an inch and a half of thick steel needle from the hand of a startled woman patient who had no idea that she was harbouring anything of the sort. I don't know who was most surprised. A number of patients were seen here, and then we ran up Sandwich Bay to Cartwright.

It was good to visit Cartwright again after seven years absence. Doctor and Mrs. Forsyth entertained us royally, and under his tutelage I took a short course in tonsil surgery under local anaesthesia, which technique I had been anxious to acquire. Miss Seabrook took notes to her heart's content and had a bonny time. It might be a good time to remark that Miss Seabrook was a most cheery and imperturbable shipmate, apparently immune to seasickness, mosquitoes, cold, wet, and a diet of fresh fish twice a day. Her study of medical services on the coast should be a penetrating and comprehensive one, too, and I hope that she will some time continue them.

After all too short a visit at Cartwright, we left late one afternoon, running out to Pack's Harbour before dark. The next morning at West Bay, we found a tragic little settlement where tuberculosis was rampant. There was nothing I could do, for I had no X-ray and there were no hospital beds available for them. I removed one child, wished them Godspeed, and went on to a port where I could be of a little more help. Some day I might be able to realize my dream of a little tuberculosis sanatorium at the head of Hamilton Inlet, and I shall feel better qualified to cope with such a situation.

We stopped at Fish Cove and then tried to enter

the tricky anchorage of Indian Island, but rocks and lack of knowledge drove us out into safer waters and we turned up Hamilton Inlet. At Ticoralak, I picked up, amongst other things, a patient with cancer of the breast, for operation at North West River, and then we ran into Rigolet at the narrow entrance to Lake Melville. Here we accumulated a quantity of freight, a deck load of gasoline in steel drums, and a number of passengers and patients. Looking like Noah's Ark, we pushed on through the narrows and into the superbly beautiful harbour at St. John's Island. Here we anchored at twilight in a lovely still harbour dominated by a 700-foot cliff crowned with birches. North West River was 50 miles up the bay from us.

The morning was crystal bright and boisterous, with a ramping westerly breeze blowing down the Bay. As we left the shelter of St. John's Island, we nearly stood on our heads. Spray flung across the bows in glittering rainbows and pelted the ship. At times she seemed almost to stop in her tracks. Sodden with our heavy deck load, we wallowed mightily, and the patients in the dispensary began to look forward to an early death by seasickness, but by noon old Mokami Mountain began to draw abeam and as we neared the head of the bay, we came to more sheltered waters.

North West River was green and pleasant under the hot sun. The gardens were prospering and the cattle fat. Jack Watts, the station superintendent, was there to welcome his medical officer home, and it was good to see him again, looking exactly the same as he did more years ago than he would care to count. My mother, who ran this large and busy station during the war years, had opened the family homestead, and I moved ashore to start on the backlog of surgery and medicine in this centre of Hamilton Inlet. A week's work included a trip to Goose Bay Airdrome, 25 miles away. We transported a number of patients up over to this Base, and the RCAF medical officer very kindly permitted them to be X-rayed in his crisp little hospital. *Maraval*'s crew watched the aircraft drift in and out of this somehow unreal airport amongst the spruce trees. Upon the completion of certain business here, we were ready to run on north.

The trip down the bay was uneventful, and we visited the ports along the north shore of Hamilton Inlet as we went. The harbours marched by, Indian Harbour, Smokey, Cut Throat, Emily Harbour, Holton, Brig Harbour, King's Harbour, and then Cape Harrison. This gloomy place had a number of schooners at anchor, and from one of them we learnt of an acutely ill man at nearby Jigger Tickle. Thither we steamed, and found a rather unusual case. The man was suffering from mosquito sandfly bites. Both eyes were closed, his head horribly swollen, his temperature was high, and he was acutely ill. Toxic reactions to flies have killed men in this country. We were able to be of considerable assistance to him.

As we ran north amongst the little Islands and ports, we found more and more fishing vessels. There were rumours of ice to the north, although these hardly prepared us for what we were to find. At Makkovik, we reached the first of the Moravian mission posts and were kindly received by the Reverend Grubb, senior.

A pleasant host we found him, and very helpful,

and I learnt that his son had joined the work and was in charge at Hopedale. At Makkovik we began to encounter Eskimos in fair numbers. Ailik was next, one of the larger fishing settlements, and then Turnavik East and West, Long Island, and Hopedale. Most of the Eskimos were out further fishing, but I met the Reverend and Mrs. Grubb, junior, and Bill and I fell to on a most interesting clinic. As Mr. Grubb explained, this and the other northern places had not had much in the way of visits from outside doctors during the war, and the burden had been entirely on the missionaries. He had many and interesting cases for us, and when we had finished the village up, he and his wife came aboard and piloted us out to Double Island, where most of the Hopedale Eskimos fish in the summer. There was a good deal to be done here. Tuberculosis was very widespread, and there were several families riddled with it. Several patients were already far beyond any possible help or hope. Many others had gross signs of the disease. In addition there was a fair variety of the usual work to be done, with one old Eskimo especially to have an enormous and disfiguring wen [boil] removed. He was absolutely delighted with the result and assured us he would have to get married again at once, having again become handsome.

There was a good number of ports in the next few days, and to enumerate them would be of little interest here. In many of them there were numerous schooners, and we learnt that the fishery was as yet uniformly bad. Most of the vessels, we heard, had gone on north, and none had been heard from since, which seemed odd.

At Nain the Reverend Peacock came aboard.

"Thank God you came," he told us. "I did indeed pray that you would. I had sent for an airplane but don't expect it will come." There was a seriously ill patient here, and it was with the greatest relief that we found we had on board the necessary equipment to relieve the condition. So often have the Moravian Missionaries done us kindnesses and services that it is deeply gratifying to be able in turn to be of some help. The Reverend Peacock, now in charge of the Moravian stations along the northern Labrador, is one of my most valued friends and advisors and an expert on the North. He and the Grand Old Man of the Labrador, the Reverend Hettasch, have done some really remarkable medical work themselves.

They rounded up all the cases in the neighbourhood, and we found about three or four days of uninterrupted work. Mrs. Peacock doubled as nurse when we wished help in removing an eye the next morning, and was a tireless assistant in the surgery. The days went by full of interest and activity, and the patient's register swelled by the hour. Both Mr. Hettasch and Mr. Peacock were keenly interested in and very well informed about the health in their district, and two more valuable or stimulating assistants could scarcely have been found. Both, of course, speak Eskimo like natives, and both know each individual personally. Mr. Peacock is a contemporary of mine as far as Labrador goes, as Mr. Hettasch was of my father's. I think no one ever leaves Nain without feeling a little better than when he arrived, and the two Missionary families and their staff become lifelong friends before one leaves. Bill Lawler and I left Nain feeling the same way, and determined to call again coming south if it could possibly be managed.

Running out of Nain, we reached Queens Lakes on a blowing wet morning, and found it full of schooners. There were, in addition, a good many Eskimos fishing there, and trade was brisk. From there on, however, we saw very few patients for several ports.

Maraval was now getting well north, and our destination was Hebron, but it was not to be. As we ran along the Kiglapait Mountains, we could see vast Cape Mugford looming into the sky, even when it was fifty miles away. It was bright and very cold, and the horizon was strangely light. "Ice," said the captain, and within an hour we were in it. Just dirty squat pans and small bergs at first, and we threaded our way through them gingerly. Along shore it looked better, and we found comparatively clear water. We met a schooner coming south, and learnt that there was much ice to the north of us. The mail schooner, a power vessel named *Winnifred Lee*, had gone north many days ago and not been heard from since. Fishing vessels were jammed into ports all along.

The land grows bold here and soars two or three thousand feet sheer out of the sea in slender spiring peaks. It is desolate country. We went on cautiously, and once were driven in by ice further than we wished to go. There was a rock in there and we hit it—hard. *Maraval* is strong and tight, but the blow was sickening and gave everybody a bad moment. She rolled heavily off the rock without even stopping, and we made a survey but could find no sign of damage, so we proceeded. The ice came ever thicker now, and the pans were larger and heavier all the time. Far out to sea it stretched as far as the eye could see. The captain watched anxiously and dodged and twisted trying to keep in the clearest possible water.

Small pans thumped against our bows from time and made the ship shiver.

It was clear, though, that the ice was closing in all the time, and finally we turned into Kiglapait Harbour, a sheltered little port where we could be protected. The harbour must be seen to be appreciated. Seven needle peaks rise sheer from the harbour in breathless tier on a high-piled tier of naked rock, slashed with patches of snow. I don't suppose the highest is over three thousand feet, but the effect is majestic beyond description. Between two of the peaks stretches one vast semicircular cliff like some great perpendicular amphitheatre. The ice moved stealthily down the coast, as far as the eye could see, and from it rose the lonely islands. Cape Mugford shimmered in the distance, looking so close that one could almost touch it, although the distance must have been over thirty miles. The huddle of schooners below the seven peaks did not look like toys, but rather, I should have said, like some sort of microbe.

Business as usual, and we learned that up the bay a few miles in another anchorage there was a schooner with a man with "pendix" [appendicitis]. Watching his chance, the captain slid out of port the next day and managed to make the other anchorage while the tide was going out and the ice had moved off briefly. The man did not need operation, and was given treatment before we returned to Kiglapait Harbour to await the withdrawal of the ice. Two fishing captains who wished to make a reconnaissance came with us as local pilots, although our captain knew the land well enough, and we ran for Cutthroat Island, which we managed to reach. The ice was thick across the entrance of the harbour, but

Captain Barbour put the little ship into it with all the skill of his years of experience, and she handled easily. Great pans, sometimes stretching shadowy and green ten or twenty feet down into the water, ground together or heaved in the swell. Leads opened and closed mysteriously, as if the whole field were moving—as indeed it was. Twice she held up motionless, but each time she was able to push the ice to either side, and at last we reached the harbour. This was free of ice when we entered, but that night, as I went aft to go to my cabin, I heard a soft whisper and hiss of water along melting ice and looked out on a whole harbour full of ice that had crept in, massive, cold, stealthy, and soundless. In the morning it had gone as silently as it has come.

The next day we threaded our way through scattered ice to a place called Moores Harbour. This was as far as we could go. My hopes of reaching Hebron had to be abandoned for 1946. The sea was one vast jam of heavy, heavy sea ice. We left Moores Harbour sadly and turned back to Cutthroat, which place we reached late in the afternoon. Here *Maraval* had a close call. We reached the end of the island about the same time as the ice coming in with the evening tide. *Maraval* altered course, and altered again, but still the ice drove in, and we were forced nearer and nearer the land. Within a hundred yards of the harbour point, it became clear that we would have a hard time to make it. Heavy floes were driving in at three or four knots. The bottom appeared, and the water shoaled rapidly. I had a hideous mental image of the little ship hurled up onto the rocks like a broken toy, with her bottom ripped out on the reefs. It was now clear we could not make it, and the captain suddenly spun the wheel over and the ship swung head on into the ice. The telegraph jingled full speed ahead, and the engine plugged heavily. There was one crash after another as she shouldered the masses of ice, some of them several times her own length, to one side. She staggered with the thrust of ice and engine but moved in through the ice, and slowly, slowly, she cleared the point on which the great floes were now grinding and thumping in a thoroughly—to me—sickening way. We were in harbour.

The next day, the sea was calm. The ice looked scattered. It was only about twenty miles to St. Jago's Bay, and the captain decided to try it. Out we went into the ice, which was indeed scattered at first, but became ever more and more close packed. Progress was slow. The captain had felt out the little ship's habits in the ice, and we were able to take on much heavier floes. Sometimes the ship would strain against a large mass for long minutes, and then slowly and ponderously it would swing aside like a door to let us on a little further. Sometimes we would run along a little lead, but always it would close in a little time. As far as the eye could see, the ice stretched, a solid field which showed open water only in streaks near at hand. At times we made a mile or less in an hour, but generally she moved along remarkably well, and it was clear that as long as things remained as they were, all would be well. Once we were nipped between two very heavy masses of ice, and the propeller was jammed, so that the engine stopped dead. We got down onto the ice and crawled in under the counter to squint at the propellor. It seemed undamaged, and we managed to push one piece of ice away. The engine started and ran well, and we sighed a deep sigh. Late in the afternoon we passed St. Jago's Bay, where we had taken shelter for a while on our way to Cutthroat, and the ice became lighter. With a sense of great relief we returned to Kiglapait Harbour and anchored under the same peaks which I had attempted, not very successfully, to scale four days before.

The next day the ice was light and we ran south at a good speed. *Maraval* had not been scratched by her week in the ice and was in good shape. At Foxy Harbour we stopped to pick up a boy with a bad hernia and proceeded to Nain.

At Nain there was still a little work to do. When this was over, we took the two missionaries with us as pilot and went to Tabor Island. This was the site of the one-time Grenfell Labradorite quarry, and I was anxious to obtain a large piece of that beautiful stone as part of a monument which the people of Labrador are erecting to my father. We spent a busy day moving a large block of stone down to the water's edge. Only sailors could have shifted that ponderous block, only sailors could ever have balanced it across beams stretched between two dories, and only sailors could have rigged all the tackles on board to swing it up onto *Maraval*'s foredeck, where it would flash green and blue whenever the spray wetted it.

The southern trip was a recapitulation of the northern one, except that North West River was not visited. Many patients were seen, and some ports missed on the way North were included. At Cartwright I abandoned the *Maraval*, which was now needed for an important task in White Bay, Newfoundland, and sent her on with Bill Lawler in charge. She made a quick run south and reached St. Mary's River in time to officiate at that station's second serious forest fire in two years. I returned to North West River for local medical work and to await *Maraval*'s return.

The main trip was over. In September I went to Cartwright to rejoin the ship, and we managed to carry a couple of cargoes up the Bay to North West River and to do a medical patrol to Hopedale and back. It was cold and stormy, and the ship went south near the end of the month.

She had seen 1,500 patients. She had transported scores of patients to hospital. We had given over 20 general anaesthetics on board, and over 40 minor surgical procedures had been performed. 950 dental extractions had been done. 150 eye tests had been made, and glasses prescribed in most cases. Much useful information had been picked up. *Maraval* was due her winter rest. When she comes back with the geese in the spring, perhaps she will have a new engine. There will be much for her to do next summer—more than there was this past one.

SOMETHING IN THE AIR

Right after his navy service in World War Two, Dad spent a bit of time in St. Anthony learning administration, as he was to be Director of Northern Medicine for the International Grenfell Association in North West River.

It was recently my pleasure to travel from North West River to St. Anthony on the American Aircraft Rescue Craft P-359. This craft has been stationed at the Goose Bay Airbase during the past summer. Her commanding officer, Lieutenant Rankin, United States Army Air Forces, has been a most kindly and considerate friend of the Mission, and it has been my pleasure to know him well personally. It was at about the time of our arrival at St. Anthony that I first gathered that he had been sent there on a most extraordinary mission. It was still shrouded in the most profound military secrecy, and as a matter of fact, Lieutenant Rankin asked me rather wistfully if I knew anything about it. It was, he said, all very obscure. In fact, he added, the prospectus was so extraordinary that he felt that for once his excellent signalmen must have made a mistake over the message. Something, he said sadly, about some kind of an airborne invasion of St. Anthony. No paratroopers, though, as he understood it. Some kind of animal, you know, and probably very ferocious, too. I gathered that Lieutenant Rankin, like the excellent officer he is, had learnt during the past few years not to waste too much time trying to fathom the minds of headquarters. If they wanted to shower northern Newfoundland with gorillas or something—well, they were going to do it and that was that. In the meantime, would I join him at luncheon?

Doctor Curtis was able to throw more light on the subject. Colonel Norman Vaughan, of the Air Sea Rescue Service, and an old friend of the Mission, had some beautiful husky dogs which were now surplus to requirements. These dogs have had distinguished war records in Europe, and had hauled wounded in Belgium during winter in certain districts where snow had made other transport impractical. They were well acquainted with the battleground and are today honoured war veterans. They were in addition fine, sturdy, young thoroughbreds and exceedingly well trained. The Colonel had wired the Mission—or rather more accurately, he had dropped a note by air—to find out if the Mission could use them. Good dogs are always needed in Labrador and northern Newfoundland, so the answer was that we would be delighted to have them. Shipping promised to be rather a problem until the colonel volunteered that he would drop them to us by parachute. Certainly—the easiest thing in the world. To men who could drop a lifeboat complete with engine to survivors floating in the sea, dropping some dogs to a northern medical Mission was more than feasible. On Sunday next . . .

Sunday was a bright blustery day, with a stiff wind whipping the harbor. The stage was set by eleven o'clock. The dog pens were prepared for guests. The largest field in St. Anthony was neatly marked with a huge white cross. Dog wardens were stationed in the more impenetrable bush around the field. Down in the harbor the big Army boat was circling vigilantly.

The majority of the village had turned out and was standing along the fenced edge of the field. Children raced around the crowd and pushed each other into ditches. Doctor Curtis strode through the crowd with his pipe surrounded by a broad grin. Fishermen, nurses, teachers, doctors, we waited with the mild bewilderment of the civilians wondering what the Armed Forces will think of next.

Right on schedule the aircraft appeared. There were two of them. One was a Douglas transport, the other a plump Catalina, and it was strange to think that her bulging hull was crammed with husky dogs. The Douglas swept low over the field for a trial run and came in again, slow and low. From her open door dropped three little parachutes, gaily colored against the crisp blue sky. There was a great rush into the bush to recover them, and three canisters were delivered to "Operations" out in the field. Two of them contained "Walkie Talkie" radio sets, and the third a Graflex camera and film. The little radio sets were quickly set up, and one was sent to a motorboat in the harbor. The other remained at HQ. The crashboat, a small motorboat, the two aircraft, and the ground crew were now linked up. The Catalina circled speculatively for a turn or two and then swept into her first "bombing run" over the field. As she passed over it, a door opened in her side, and from it blossomed a gay parachute with a startled husky dog swinging below, dropping fast but not fast enough. He was borne across the field and went streaking over the village like a hound of the Baskervilles to splash miserably into the frigid harbour water.

The plane was coming in for her second run by the time he had been rescued and brought shivering to the field. He was a big, handsome brute of an Alaskan-type sled dog, very similar to our own stock. Wet and bedraggled as he was, he had not entirely lost his composure, and with his deep chest and broad shoulders he made a fine sight. In the meantime the aircraft was making her second run. This one yielded two parachutes, a crimson one and a bright blue one, and their passengers went spinning down, swinging slowly, into the dense brushwood below the field. They too, joined headquarters in the field. Not greatly upset by their drop, they were none the less so delighted to be on solid ground that they were literally trying to dig their way into it. Each dog, we found, had a tag around his neck with his name and a line about his characteristics. "Tanney, shy but a good hauler," was one; "Chinook, good trail dog," was another.

By now the plane was getting the range and only one other dog landed in the water. Two landed together near the Mission barn, one of them crashing full into a fence but apparently not in the least hurt by his crash landing. Accuracy became very good, and the last dog landed on the edge of the target area, close to where we were standing. The field was becoming gay with parachutes of red and blue and yellow and white, looking like giant flowers in the hard bright sunshine. Finally, the last dog had—we presume—shouted "Geronimo" in true paratrooper fashion, gritted his teeth, and bailed out to a safe landing. The two planes came over for a farewell wave. In one of them was Major Eddie Goodale, former WOP [volunteer], St. Anthony and North West River, and lately with the Air Sea Rescue service. The planes circled and then wheeled south towards home. In a minute they were vanishing specks.

The dogs were lined up: eight big, powerful huskies with their bushy tails jauntily curled over their backs. They made a magnificent sight, and one could visualize them as they will be this winter, a cheerful, eager team who will carry the doctor and his medical box to uncounted homes in lonely hamlets by the silent frozen harbours and runs. They had accepted their hectic morning with the cheerful composure of the true husky and were ready for anything. They were duly photographed, and Lieutenant Rankin then formally presented them to Doctor Curtis as a present from the US Army Air Forces to the Grenfell Mission.

The whole affair seemed somehow fitting and appropriate. Only a few weeks before, the US Army Air Force had dropped the colossal bombs which had ended the war, and now they were to be seen engaged in this somehow implausible and perhaps incredible enterprise which represented anything but the conventional sort of military act. The whole business had been a little bewildering, but it had represented a truly kindly and constructive thought as well as a beautiful and valuable gift. Long after history has decided the arguments about Tokyo policy, the posterity of Tanney (shy but a good hauler) and his aerial shipmates will be serving the traveller and the settler, the doctor and the nurse of the coast. I hope that for a long time to come they will haul the doctor on his winter rounds, with his long travelling komatik and the battered box with its red cross. Perhaps in days to come the toiling team will look up at some peaceful aircraft, penciling its vapour trail across the winter sky, and remember that, back in '45, they too did a bit of flying.

DOG TEAMS

In the winter of 1912, Harry started doing medical patrols by dog team. These trips went as far north as Hebron and as far south as Mary's Harbour and measured anywhere between 1,000 and 2,000 miles. They took a toll on Harry's body, and I believe they were in some measure responsible for his premature death in 1939 at the young age of 58. After returning from his naval service in World War Two, Tony spent twelve winters covering the same area in much the same way. Things hadn't changed much, and the trips were very long and very challenging physically. It was a rare day when doctor or driver rode on the komatik, and the usual drill was to run or walk alongside to lighten the load for the dogs. Tony ranged even farther north than his father and spent a night in a stone house near Saglek on one occasion.

Things had improved after the war due to the introduction of reliable air travel. The Royal Canadian Air Force was authorized to do "mercy flights" and would always stretch the definition to help out the Grenfell Mission. The usual drill was to fly Tony north to Nain or perhaps Hebron, at which point he would hire a succession of local teams and drivers for the weeks-long return trip to North West River. In 2012, I was regaled with stories by Bert Winters, who lived in Makkovik then but who has since passed on. Bert was one of Tony's drivers and it was a treat to listen to him.

In 1957, the Newfoundland Government agreed to pay for an air ambulance stationed in North West River, and this revolutionized the provision of health care in Labrador.

Tony was more than glad to give up the dog team trip. I have a letter to that effect, written to a young doctor who was hoping to do such trips while working for the Mission.

I have accounts of five dog team medical patrols and have included them here along with some other dog stories. The first one is included in Labrador Doctor, *but I thought it would be nice to have them all in one volume. The reader will note that that trip lasted from December 19 to May 1. Tony hardly ever included dates in his writing. A bit of an annoying oversight. I have assigned a year to each account based on corroborating (but not conclusive) evidence.*

Dog team travel was often hard work but usually interesting. The dogs themselves were a never-ending source of interest and sometimes amusement. They seemed to love their work though heaven knew why, and were wildly excited while being harnessed in the morning, yelping, howling, leaping up and down, eager to be off. They accepted the rope or skin line harnesses with good grace, bent their heads down as the harness slid over head and neck, allowed their front paws to be lifted and dropped through the proper place. The harnesses were always dried completely or as much as possible overnight, for if wet they would chafe badly and even cut through fur and skin. They were large animals, as a rule, many the size of a big Alsatian, but with much thicker fur and bushy tails which were curled tightly over their backs unless they were in pain or disastrously fatigued. Most had a jaunty air of confidence. During the yelling and jumping up and down of being harnessed, they watched for a chance to get a nip at each other and there was a good deal of what could only have been bad language, but once it was time to go, they strained eagerly, waiting for the word. The komatik would be loaded before the dogs were harnessed, and for me a typical load would consist of a large grub box, usually in front on the deck of the komatik and serving as a seat for the driver when he was not running alongside, and behind it in varied order two sleeping bags in their canvas sacks, a good-sized medicine chest, other cases including an eye outfit with a case of test lenses, boxes of eyeglasses, etc., and a dental kit for extractions. South of the timber line, one would carry a tent and a small sheet metal camp stove, a simple rectangular box in which the three lengths of 3-foot stovepipe are carried, and small cases of extra food, a dog-feed tub and feed for the dogs, and of course axe, rifle, and various spare equipment. There was usually a black bear skin to cover the boxes, so that when the whole load is lashed to the komatik bars with the rather elastic sealskin line, the bear fur provides a warm upholstery tied firmly down to the box. Eight really good dogs can haul just about anything you put on the komatik, and (in good conditions) driver and doctor. In fact, if it is cold, one gets off and runs at regular intervals for warmth. If the going is bad, the snow being very deep or very crusty or very wet, no one rides, and in deep snow, one or two go ahead of the dogs, breaking trail on snowshoes.

Father was often away during the winter, and his longest trip would be northward to Nain and back, a journey which would take six weeks or more. It was said that he preferred to run all day, which kept him comfortably warm, and he was immensely strong and quite unfreezable. He tried to visit each house in the isolated hamlets. His drivers—there were only two or three in many years—were remarkable men, and Jim Pottle who lived out on the coast near Flatwater Brook was particularly so. He exerted perfect discipline over his team, which was actually owned by the International Grenfell Association. Feeding a team of husky dogs was something of an adventure, for they ate but once a day, usually in the evening or whenever they finished their day's work and were unharnessed, and were always hungry. There was much competition to be first into the feed tub, and arguments could be lethal, for the husky dog has formidable teeth. Jim was one of the few drivers who could get his dogs to arrange themselves in front of him in a sort of semicircle, quivering with eagerness, while he tossed each one a piece of seal meat or fat, or a herring or whatever was available. The others would remain motionless. Fights and robberies were simply not on. Each dog got his morsel and could eat it in peace. Feeding time could otherwise turn into a bloody carnage on occasion, especially when the meal was one of cooked feed. This was served out in tubs cut out of old barrels, and consisted of pieces of seal meat, blubber, chunks of herring, dried capelin, or on rare occasions whale meat, cooked in a sort of porridge of corn meal. On the trail, one tried not to cook, as it involved building a fire and hanging pots over it, often in freezing weather, until they boiled, but in the home village, it was the most economical feed. A gentle and good natured man, Jim understood his charges perfectly, and they him. They knew that he could put out a candle or cut a cigarette in half at 30 feet with his driver's whip of braided sealskin thong tapering to a single strand, or cut an inch or two of hair and hide off an offender, and sometimes it was necessary when dog fights broke out, for they could easily kill each other. They were, however, fun-loving, amiable creatures most of the time, played practical jokes on amateur drivers, were gifted thieves if there were edibles on the komatik, and would literally work themselves to utter exhaustion for someone who handled them properly.

There were few in-patients in the hospital at North West River, because only a very small number of Labrador people lived near enough to get to it in case of illness, being carried in a "coach box," which was a sort of box lashed to the komatik, in which a patient could lie on furs or bedding and be well covered, though he would take a good jolting in rough going. The komatik was a wooden sled, from twelve to twenty-two feet long, up to two feet wide, with steel or occasionally whale bone or even plastic shoeing on the runners. The deck was made of cross slabs called bars, perhaps four or five inches wide, projecting out over the runner on both sides, and the load could be lashed to the outer ends of these bars. They were not nailed or screwed on, but lashed with stout fishing line, which went through drilled holes in the bars and the runners. These lashings gave great flexibility to the whole sled, so that it could give, resisting violent stress. The runners could bend an inch out of line from the vertical, and the whole thing moved as if it was made of rubber. Any other arrangement tended to break up on rough ice or bad going, but the komatik slithered along with its own shock absorbing system built into it.

The load was arranged so that the most needed objects—gun, grub box and primus stove if in the treeless northern area—could be got at quickly. I myself liked to carry a good pocket compass, and found it extremely useful in thick weather, though drivers—who almost always knew exactly where they were—tended to regard this as an eccentricity. On several occasions, however, the compass was right, and a driver like Sam Broomfield, who served with me several years and was one of the finest pilots ever, became quite tolerant of this frill. He was impressed with how precisely one could run a course with a compass, even in darkness and during snow. One other habit is worth mentioning, and this is the practice of putting all medicinal ampoules and vials into the foot of one's sleeping bag, along with a couple of tins containing 50 glass carpoules with rubber stoppers. Most such containers could freeze, usually cracking the container, and the carpoules would break the seals at either end when frozen, rendering the contents unsterile. Kept in the sleeping bag all day, the warm down filling prevented them from freezing, and in a snowhouse or in a very cold building, they were left at the foot of the bag all night, warmed by the doctor.

Again and again, when disaster struck and some driver froze to death, as sometimes happens, if he lost his way in drifting snow and wandered out on the sea on the ice or otherwise ran out of warmth and strength, his team would usually lie around the komatik, patiently waiting. They would never touch his sealskin clothing—rated about like caviar to a husky—or tear open the boxes on the komatik until a rescue team came. Alas, it was customary at one time to shoot all dogs of a team whose driver had perished, no matter how faithful their vigil. Only once in my life did I ever feel afraid of a dog team—not my own—and indeed that event very nearly cost me my life, but of that, more later. Mostly the dogs were good working companions to their human masters, affable, patient, wonderfully strong and willing to work as long as they could stand up. Father loved his dearly, though he never petted one in the presence of the rest, as it would instantly cause a wild attack by jealous teammates on the favoured animal, but when not at work, as in the summer, the dogs were as friendly and gentle as any other dogs, often deeply affectionate.

Interestingly enough, many of the leaders were females, and in the very masculine society of the day the drivers would only tell those they knew personally that this was because they were just as smart, more attentive, and never got into fights. The male lead dog was usually a big powerful animal, and though he knew his work quite well he had to defend his seniority continually and was apt to injure other dogs or to end up crippled. The females were treated with a good deal of respect and never ever fought, and in my view they were better at memorizing geography than the male, being perfectly capable of following a long intricate trail for a day or two on end with no help if they had done it once the previous year.

The komatik always started off at a dead run, but the dogs soon thought better of that and settled down to the speed compatible with surface conditions. They were tremendously eager, would pull almost till they dropped, tended faithfully to business, and seemed to enjoy it. Making pets of the dogs while they were working was very bad practice and always aroused jealousies and damaging injuries. Our own children and those of my brother were allowed to play outside among the beautiful pure white dogs my brother bred in North West River, and the six or seven dogs watched over these small children with great gentleness and would not allow any other dogs near them. A strange team of visiting dogs might well have been dangerous, but the matched crew of exceptionally big strong animals were good watchdogs, and were quite devoted to their owners. Two were my own (five belonging to my brother) and had traveled great distances as additions to the teams I hired, and though they took no sauce from the other dogs they were extremely good-natured, magnificent workers and coveted by most of my drivers. Such beautiful and devoted animals were, alas, short lived, for they worked hard and were subject to severe hardships, and a sled dog was past his prime at six, and rarely lived another two or three years. They were extraordinarily affectionate when not working, endlessly entertaining and anxious to please. They were also obedient and disciplined, though they rarely experienced any physical punishment from us. Their own social usages and behaviour in the community of dogs would warrant a book in itself, but despite the streak of Arctic wolf and probably of Siberian and Samoyed, they were an endless source of pleasure and as close to us as two species can be.

LIBERATOR, A GIFT FROM ABOVE

Retold by Dave Paddon. I based this story on the short reference to the incident in Dad's book as well as talks with my cousin. He was a volunteer in North West River with the International Grenfell Association, and Dad told him the story in much greater detail. He never talked about it with me or any of my siblings. I also referred to the original United States Air Force accident report but did not quote from it.

Every cloud has a silver lining, and it's hard to say how many Labradorians benefited from this incident. This is a story about a great medical breakthrough in Labrador. It involved tragedy for a small number of individuals but a wonderful benefit to a much larger number. My father never told me this story, but he did relate it to my cousin who passed it on to me. It gets a brief mention in his autobiography but is worthy, I think, of a volume of its own. I have, out of necessity, inferred a fair amount and drawn my own conclusions based on research as well as conversations with Labradorians who remember the incident.

I'll start this story in 1912 when my grandparents, Harry Paddon and Mina Gilchrist, arrived on the coast of Labrador as doctor and nurse with the International Grenfell Association. They were posted to Indian Harbour, where they ran a small cottage hospital catering to the needs of the local livyere [year-round resident] population as well as the crews of the schooners which came north from Newfoundland each year to prosecute the northern cod fishery. Hundreds of vessels would show up each summer with a few months to "make their voyage" and then return to Newfoundland for the winter. Indian Harbour was strategically located midway along the coast, and in addition to the hospital there were various fishing enterprises located there.

Fishing was a hazardous business, and Harry and Mina were confronted with numerous puncture and knife wounds, strains and sprains, and the ubiquitous "water pups," blisters caused by the constant chafing of coarse oil clothes. They were mainly on the neck and wrists and could become infected. Antibiotics were far off in the future, and careful medical care was required. In addition there was a huge amount of tuberculosis back then as well as nutritional diseases like scurvy, beriberi, and rickets. All in all it was a pretty grim picture, and the new doctor and nurse were very busy.

Harry and Mina got married in 1913, and my father, Tony, showed up soon after, the first of four brothers.

Indian Harbour would close down in the fall after the last schooners had headed south, and the newly married Paddons were told to go to Mud Lake, 150 miles west in central Labrador, and set up another medical outpost in an abandoned lumber camp. In 1915 they moved the winter operation to North West River. They got there in *Yale*, a 40-foot auxiliary ketch which served the International Grenfell Association for many years and was perhaps Harry's second love, as he covered the Labrador coast in her for many years.

In the winter of 1912, Harry started doing long dog team trips which would last for many weeks. He would go as far north as Hebron and south to Mary's Harbour, covering somewhere between a thousand and two thousand miles and visiting every homestead in every bay or inlet and seeing the entire populace. These trips were physically very demanding and took a considerable toll on the body. It was a rare thing to actually ride on the komatik as it was always heavily loaded and the snow and ice conditions were seldom ideal. Harry or his driver would walk or trot alongside of the komatik for hours and often had to go ahead on snowshoes to break a trail for the dogs. By the age of 55 Harry had been doing these trips for 25 years, and he began to have health problems.

The year 1939 was a sabbatical year for Harry and Mina, and they were in the northeastern US where their sons were at school, Tony being in medical school in New York. The six of them were planning a Christmas together, but it was not to be. On Christmas Eve 1939, worn out and frail from 27 years of dog team trips, Harry suffered an acute bacterial infection and peritonitis set in. Antibiotics were new then, having been identified only about ten years before, and were not generally available. It's quite possible that they would have saved Harry's life, but it was not to be and he succumbed after a couple of days.

After the dust had settled, Mina went back to North West River to run the hospital, along with nurse Florence Goudie. They were on their own for all of World War Two, the only doctor in Labrador being stationed in Cartwright, about 150 miles away.

As soon as the ink was dry on Tony's medical diploma, he joined the Royal Canadian Naval Volunteer Reserve and soon found himself on corvette escort ships shepherding convoys back and forth across the Atlantic. It was a busy time for a ship's doctor with lots of torpedoes and lots of ships sunk, which produced lots of survivors with lungs often full of salt water and fuel oil. Tony was assigned to *HMCS Guysborough* for the Normandy invasion and found himself sweeping mines in channel 2 at Omaha beach on June 6, 1944. The ship was torpedoed and sunk on March 17, 1945, and 50 men were lost. Tony was lucky enough to have been transferred to *HMCS Teme* and so missed that unfortunate incident. However his luck ran out 12 days later on March 29, when *Teme* was torpedoed. Four men were lost and the rearmost 60 feet of the ship was blown off. What was left of the ship was towed into Penzance Harbour and subsequently declared a write-off. The war ended a few weeks later, and Tony found himself on a small passenger liner going west... with the lights on.

On returning to North West River, Tony was warmly welcomed by his mother, as was his brother, my uncle Dick, whose motor torpedo boat had also been blown up by a mine during the war. She was glad to have her boys back and was also exhausted from running the hospital for the last five years or so.

Much of the progress in health care that had been made before the war had been undone. Tuberculosis was rampant, and nutritional diseases plus high infant and maternal mortality were widespread. Tony took over the running of the eight-bed hospital, which often had 20 or more in patients, and set out to get things back on track.

One day in the early summer of 1945, he was walking home to our old house near North West River's beautiful sandy beach when a small boy ran up to him and thrust out a hand in which he held a shiny glass object. "What's this, Doctor?"

Tony's reaction was one of shock and amazement. He knew what he was looking at but he couldn't believe his eyes. I'd like to leave that scene temporarily, but try to picture it in your mind. A young boy clutching... something! A startled doctor bent over and staring in total disbelief.

Many will know that during World War Two, large numbers of allied aircraft were assembled in North America and then ferried over to the UK for the war effort. Most of these went through Gander in Newfoundland, Goose Bay in Labrador, or Frobisher Bay [Iqaluit] in Nunavut. Every day huge numbers of mostly four-engine bombers would arrive or depart these stations on their way to Keflavik, Iceland to refuel prior to the final hop to Britain. Due to the demands of war, the level of pilot experience was very low, and accidents were common. It wasn't unusual for a pilot to have perhaps 400 hours flying time, and this was very little for what they faced in heavily laden B24s and B17s with engines that were not very reliable by today's standards. I flew airplanes for 40 years, and I can say that when I had that level of experience, I was flying a small, single-engine airplane in the daylight, in good weather, and with perhaps three or four passengers. If everything went just right, these 20-something-year olds could just about get across the ocean and on to the war-torn skies over Germany. If something went wrong, they could be quickly overwhelmed.

And so it was that on the night of January 13, 1945, according to my research, a B24 Liberator under the command of Captain Roger J. Mellion departed Goose Bay for the long haul to Iceland. It didn't get far. According to US Air Force accident records, something went wrong and the airplane crashed on the frozen surface of Lake Melville just six miles from the runway. Mellion and his eight crewmates were all killed. It wasn't an unusual occurrence during the war. Things quickly got back to normal afterwards, with hostilities ending a few months later.

Now come back with me to what I like to think was a lovely early summer day in North West River. Early June, perhaps, although I don't know the precise date. A little boy is holding up a shiny object, and a flabbergasted doctor is bent over trying to articulate his thoughts. "Where did you get that?!"

"On the beach, Doctor. There's all kinds of them lying around in the landwash."

I imagine Dad taking off for North West River's beautiful sandy beach with the little fellow chasing along behind, wondering what the heck was going on.

When Dad got to the beach he got what I imagine was the second biggest shock of his life, after being torpedoed a few months earlier. Dozens of the things were lying around at his feet, and more were coming in on the tide. Dad started filling his pockets and told the boy to go and get all his friends and pick up as many as they could. He would give them a penny each for them. Not bad money in those days. Not long after that a prize was instituted for whoever could bring in the most. It was won by Sandy Rich, whom I remember very well. Dick Budgell told me he remembered picking them up, as did Jean Crane. They were both living in North West River then.

I don't know the exact circumstances, but I imagine Dad standing on the beach and looking intently at one of these little things. No doubt he was thinking that if he'd had one six years ago, he could have saved his own father's life. Because you see, what he held in his hand was a vial of penicillin: the very latest wonder drug that, at the time, was being used only by Allied militaries to treat wounded service personnel. Antibiotics were still new at the time and were referred to as "miracle drugs" due to their amazing efficacy against bacterial infections. As a nurse in London during the war, my mother gave injections of the new medicine to wounded men with terrible infections. The results were amazing, and men would go from the point of death to sitting up in bed in a few hours.

Roughly 400 of the little vials were eventually gathered, and they were put to use right away. One of the first to benefit was a little girl named Stephanie Peacock whom I had the great pleasure of interviewing a couple of years ago. She's a retired school teacher living in Gander now, but in 1945 she was living in Nain with her missionary parents. She told me that one day she walked into Nain harbour, which was freezing cold, and that she came down with pneumonia not long after. She was in very serious condition when Dad happened along on a medical patrol. I'm not sure what time of year it was, but when doing dog team patrols Dad would keep a small metal box full of vials inside his parka to prevent them from freezing. Stephanie got a shot of penicillin, and a few hours later she was sitting up asking for something to eat.

Dad used every one of the vials, continuing to do so until well after supplies of antibiotics became more readily available. They were simply too precious to throw away, and he was still using them in the early 1950s.

I'll conclude the story by asking the reader to take a moment and think of Captain Mellion and his crew of eight. The oldest man aboard the doomed B24 Liberator was, I believe, 28. Mellion himself was 22, and his logbook, recovered at the crash site, revealed a total of 436 hours of flight time. Pitifully low. Those young men never made it to the great fight against totalitarianism, but they did make a huge difference to the people of Labrador. Because you see, dear reader, their aircraft had been carrying some medical freight to Europe, including the vials of penicillin that washed up on the beach at North West River a few months later. Liberator indeed.

I should make it clear that I cannot say for certain that Mellion's aircraft was carrying the penicillin. The information that I got was that the drugs had indeed come from a B24, three of which crashed near Goose Bay in the winter of 1944-45. But the other two crashed on land. Mellion's airplane came down about 20 miles from Goose Bay on the same body of water as North West River. It would seem that when the ice melted in the spring, the aircraft sank, and the vials were somehow released, drifted for a while, and eventually washed ashore.

BUTTER AND SNOW HOUSE CALL

Retold by Dave Paddon. Based on the story I got from Tony Paddon and a chat with Tommy Watt.

Butter and Snow is as picturesque as it sounds. About three miles from North West River, it was inhabited by the Ritch family for many years and was one of many small settlements which contained only one or two families.

In the early 1990s, I was living in Edmonton and somehow discovered that Tommy Watt lived about a ten-minute walk from me. Quite the coincidence. I asked Tommy if I could interview him for *Them Days* magazine, and he agreed on the condition that I play racquetball with him. He was twice my age but I could barely get a point off him. I remember him as having a shock of white hair and a pencil moustache and thinking he just needed a silk scarf and leather jacket to look every inch the dashing World War Two pilot.

He was quite the character and told me that he and Dad were always playing jokes on each other. On one occasion they were in Nain, and Dad was presented with an arctic hare. They were caught for weather for a few days, and Tommy decided he wanted a meal of hare. He carefully preserved the skin of the animal and then stuffed it full of old rags, batteries and bits of wire. Not long after Dad returned from Nain, a meal of hare was planned at the Paddon residence. I guess it was leftovers that night.

Not long after this incident, Tommy happened to purchase a nice new sleeping bag. Not long after the acquisition a horrible smell started to issue from the bag. It turned out that Dad had put some capelin down in the foot of it, and the bag was ruined. Evens, I suppose. This story was told to me many years ago by either my mother or my father as well as by Tommy Watt, whom I will introduce shortly. It must have happened in the early 1950s and involved a house call at Butter and Snow. This beautifully named location was a small enclave of one or two families about five miles east of North West River, Labrador, and I think everyone there was named Ritch. The patriarch of the little community was Fred Ritch and he had a large family.

One day in mid-winter, Fred was not feeling too well. He dispatched his son Sandy—whom I remember very well—to North West River to fetch the doctor. Sandy harnessed his dogs and took off immediately and with a great sense of urgency. Father was sick after all. The dogs were in good shape, so it didn't take too long to cover the distance to town, and Sandy was soon pounding on the door of the doctor's house in a state of some agitation. My mother responded, and Sandy told her the doctor was needed at Butter and Snow, and that it was an emergency. My father was still at the hospital but expected home shortly. Sandy promptly departed for home again, and I suppose that in his state of excitement he didn't give much thought as to how the doctor was going to make the trip.

My father arrived home shortly after and got the message about Fred. He must have been a little curious as to why Sandy hadn't waited for him, but he was used to walking long distances on snowshoes during winter medical patrols, so he grabbed a few things and set off for Butter and Snow. I suppose he must have had a bit of supper first.

Not too long after that, Tommy Watt showed up at the doctor's house. Tommy was a pilot with Wheeler Airlines and was stationed in North West River that winter. I think he must have been flying supplies to exploration camps, but he also did the odd medevac for the Grenfell Mission, which didn't have a dedicated aircraft at the time. His Norseman aircraft was on skis, and he operated from the beach and lived in what would later become Zack and Ruby Tuttauk's house. He was in the habit of coming over for a cup of coffee in the evenings, and he and my father were good friends as well as great pranksters who liked to victimize each other. Tommy had flown bombers in World War Two and had been shot down.

Tommy breezed into the house and asked where the doctor was. My mother told him what had happened, and he quickly decided that the my father shouldn't have to do all that walking when there was a perfectly good airplane available. My mother pointed out that it was now well after dark, but that didn't bother Tommy.

It was indeed too dark to fly, but it wasn't too dark to taxi, now, was it? Tommy went down to the beach, fired up the old Norseman, and set off across the bay following my father's snowshoe track with the help of his landing light. It didn't take too long for Tommy to catch up, and I can only imagine my father's surprise to see the Norseman bouncing along and getting closer and closer. Tommy eventually found the man he was looking for, pulled up beside him, and offered a ride. My father must have been greatly amused, but he jumped aboard, and Tommy proceeded to taxi all the way to Butter and Snow. Not very far, really, and I wonder if he went between Pork and Green Islands or out around?

The inhabitants of Butter and Snow must have been a little surprised, I suppose. They didn't get too many aircraft in, and certainly none at night. There was nothing seriously wrong with Fred, and after a cup of tea, Tommy and the doctor concluded the house call and taxied the five miles or so back to North West River. All in a day's work in those days, I suppose, and it sure makes a good story 70 years along.

WINTER MEDICAL PATROL, 1946-47

December 17. Sandwich Bay is beginning to freeze. Proposing to start in two days, going north to Hamilton Inlet and up this long bay to North West River, thence to nearby Goose Bay, whence the Royal Canadian Air Force will fly me 250 miles north to Nain. Thence shall work south by dog team, back to Cartwright and on as far south as possible towards the Quebec border.

December 19. My driver, Ken Webber of Spotted Islands, and I start this morning with a heavy load and bad going conditions. Can only manage about three miles an hour. Bitterly cold, clear. Sandwich Bay not safely frozen, we have to go far up the bay to cross. Pass a few patients on the way, stopping also to give diphtheria toxoid—there is an epidemic on the coast this winter—and drive on out toward North River. Shoot a partridge just before sunset.

Arrive long after dark, after long roundabout trip, can see the lights of Cartwright only nine miles across the bay, though we have driven over 30. Number of patients to be seen. Up once at 2 am for patient with violent paroxysm of asthma. Slept well, my eider sleeping bag very good. In this work one learns to spread one's sleeping bag in any vacant stretch of floor and sleep comfortably right on the bare boards, lying so that there is no pressure on any bony point. What I do dislike about sleeping on floors is the house dust, some of which, in this country, must contain a good many tubercule bacilli.

December 20. Up three hours before daybreak. Usual bread and tea, which one sees three or four times a day, I add a tin of herring from our stocks. Very cold, the snow is very dry and sandy and the komatik does not run easily, pulls sullenly, snow groans and creaks dismally under runners, dogs pull patiently without enthusiasm.

Very cold, I must run to keep warm, running is difficult as I sink a foot through the hard snow at each step. Severe frost, brisk wind—a bad combination. I generally find it necessary to work on my face with my hands about each three or four minutes to prevent freezing, have never found decent solution to problem that hands seldom warm up between exposures. Sealskin boots not quite big enough, tight, must run most of time to keep from freezing feet—very annoying.

Cross North River portage, drop onto the Strand, vast sandy beach stretching 30 miles, almost to Hamilton Inlet. Steep sand dunes on left, on right the lonely grey sea, skimming over with thickening snow and bits of ice, surging on a most desolate shore. No life of any sort. Pass 20 miles of recent burn from severe forest fire, only dead skeletons of trees. I have wrenched a knee, running, begins to bother me. Rough going, frozen hummocks of spray and sand, difficult at times

Day wears away, twilight very lonely and darkness comes with no prospect of making our destination. There is a tilt or log cabin at Woody Point, a mile before one leaves the Strand, we plan to camp there. In dark we go past it, grind wearily on an hour before finding our mistake, then turn back, myself full of thoughts on being a medical missionary which cannot be recorded here.

We find the tilt, it is buried in snow. Dogs exhausted, Ken and I tired and fed up, there is no dry wood at Woody Point, we must try to burn green. The stove pipe has rusted through and collapsed, we go coughing out into the frost. Together we attack the stove pipe again, thank heavens we get it propped up somehow, then the stove takes a deep breath and slowly begins to turn red hot. Rock-hard skin boots thaw out, snow melts on clothing, the damp little cave of a place begins to be warm and cheerful. Candle stumps stuck to the logs and lighted, then we cook a large and very hot stew of tinned meat, venison, biscuits—anything we can find in the box. After supper Ken and I build a fire outside, cook supper for our dog team—ten rather small husky dogs. Then into sleeping bags, to be awakened once in the crackling frost by a furious dog fight, sounds of most blood-curdling nature. None of dogs killed, can't help wishing there had been.

December 21. Frosty, blowing hard, dry going. Rabbit Brook at 10 am, Planter's Bight nearby. Much tuberculosis in these settlements, other cases as well, do what we can and depart, leaving at noon for Flatwater, where three families live at the mouth of a large brook renowned for the trout and smelt caught there all winter. Our host, Job

Williams, hasn't much, but what he has is gladly offered. His wife fried trout for us until the whole family was watching, fascinated at our capacity. In Labrador, most of these little one or two room houses get very cold at night after the kitchen stove goes out. This one, I think, much colder than outdoors.

December 22. Up at 5:30. Tin of beans, bread and tea. Harness our dogs by flashlight, with stiff fingers, start off in pitch dark. As result, go up wrong brook, losing a whole hour. On right way, we head across the ten mile portage separating the sea, at Flatwater, from the bottom of Back Bay, a 35 mile cul-de-sac of Lake Melville (the upper basin of Hamilton Inlet). Back Bay runs southeast almost to the sea, and I think it was once the original entrance to Lake Melville. It has an evil name amongst winter travellers.

As we cross the neck sky becomes overcast, air much warmer, few snowflakes, then more, and we realize a southeaster is brewing. We drop to the ice of Back Bay, about noon, after hard crossing, and there it reaches, stretching as far as the eye can see into the hazy distance, barren shores with occasional skirts of low woods. No house or shelter for 25 miles. Begins to snow heavily. There is rough ice—rough ice in Labrador means that the first ice broke up before an autumn gale. Millions of ice pans, forced vertically by pressure, freeze in a matrix of wet snow and young ice. Even walking through it is difficult, we can manage a mile an hour, but by swinging close to south shore we find it smoother, crawl up to a triumphant 2 or 2.5.

Snow and wind increase, the landscape blots out, we continue. Cannot stop to eat, we have a tin of frozen sardines and a biscuit, clumsily cut my finger to the bone, it bleeds all afternoon, soaking my mitten which freezes stickily. Ken and I take turns going ahead to pick out the smoothest path, the dogs follow wearily. Five hours later it is getting dark, we swing in near shore as there are signs of dangerous ice. Shore looms dimly through drift, the wind roars, we can recognize nothing. Doubt that we have passed the house we had hoped to reach. Going is frightful, the dogs spent—thank heaven the wind is behind us instead of in our faces. My knee worse and worse.

At last we give up, make camp in a little skirt of trees. Looks dismal, but Ken is a good woodsman and the tent is soon pitched on a floor of fir boughs laid over packed snow, and the tin stove set up. Plenty of dry wood nearby. No water, we melt snow. Tent soon cozy, smell of coffee and of cooking partridge, outside the gale roars. Let it! Poor dogs, cooking for them impossible at present, they get small ration of frozen seal each and curl up patiently in the snow, are soon buried.

December 23. Blowing wildly and drifting. We break camp. Ken whistles for his dogs, who rise suddenly from the snow which has completely buried most of them. The right call, I reflect, can always summon strength and eagerness out of this apparently desolate wilderness. We stumble on in smothering drift for hour or two, come to another house, Hugh Palliser, an Eskimo from Rigolet district. He and his wife kind hosts. Family faced with starvation, hunting unsuccessful, no more food. We leave a little. Wait 24 hours, get away at daybreak, the 24th.

December 24. Drifting heavily, this time from the west, clear and cold, we go along fairly well. See fresh track of team in snow, realize we are catching up with Steve MacDonald, fur trader of Cartwright, who left for North West River several hours ahead of us on the 19th. We overtake him at noon, have lunch with him at a little tilt in Pease Cove, where the two little houses are now both deserted. Pushing on all afternoon we reach Sandy Cove at dusk, a picturesque little cove under the great lowering hills of eastern Lake Melville. Patients to see, a fresh venison supper.

December 25. Christmas day. Drifting, very cold, we cross Lake Melville gingerly, aware ice not yet safe. For three nights I have dreamed of going through ice and drowning, hope not prophetic. Ice very rough, but seems safe enough and we get safely across to Valley's Bight, where both teams stop for a lunch. Patient to be seen. Then up shore through rough ice along the dark highlands, long hours of slow painful progress, we reach the lowlands tilt an hour after dusk. Steve has been there an hour—his dogs are faster than ours—tilt is snug and warm and cleaned out. The two drivers cook for dogs, we go to bed. All night the 19 dogs prowl up and down snarling or growling deep rumbling growls, occasional wild clamour, the drivers must dash out to try to prevent death of some of our dogs. Bitterly cold, night is gorgeous outside.

December 26. Long slow passage, all day, reach Mulligan Point at twilight, we are only 26 miles from North West River. I have killed a good deal of meat during the day, there is great sparring back and forth between the occupants of the two tents about a supper invitation. Of course we will share partridges, but we feign selfishness, there is much apprehension in other tent. A gift of an onion and some pork just before supper is ignored, the smell of fresh partridge is driving the other party wild. At last we relent. All of us gorged on the fresh meat, the two tents very snug. Gorgeous northern lights, piercingly cold. Trees crackle in frost. Dogs cold, tried to sleep on tent, nearly collapsing it. Bitter but beautiful morning. I leave Steve two hours after starting, going to Salt Pond, where see patients and visit my brother who has house there.

December 28. Reached North West River, place looks cold, our cattle nearly frozen to death, thank heavens we are getting new barn summer 1947. Busy here for few days, make a short trip around upper part of Bay, giving toxoid and seeing patients. Miss Omerod, station nurse, also hard at work on toxoid. Much dentistry etc.

January 19. To Goose Bay. Plane not ready, weather poor.

January 26. Group Captain Leigh, Commanding Officer Royal Canadian Air Force at Goose flying me himself, Flight Lieutenant Hartman co-pilot. Royal Canadian Air Force most charming hosts, am thoroughly delighted with genuine interest of the service in welfare of the country, they are always of great assistance to us, eager to do anything useful. As ex-officer I am most impressed by level of officers and men at Goose. Flight to Nain lasted 2 hours 10 minutes. All my gear landed on ice, plane had to return to Goose almost immediately.

Very good to see the Hettasch and Peacock families at Nain, the Moravian missionaries are friends of many years standing. Reverend Peacock and I went to work at once. Large and busy clinic for three days without a break, also a hundred-odd dental extractions, numerous minor surgical procedures, all the children to be toxoided against diphtheria. After three days, ready to leave. Dogs are dying of a mysterious "dog sickness" which periodically sweeps the North. Some evidence that this is an epidemic distemper, so Bill Peacock and I send wires and get government interested in providing enough serum for 2,000 dogs. It will be quite a job giving it. Government very cooperative as usual.

January 30 to February 9. Steady warm weather, pelting rain or snow or both, impossible to leave.

February 9. Must go anyway, sick with frustration, very worried about long delay north. Two Eskimo drivers and 14 dogs and enormous komatik. While waiting six of my dogs died, got two or three more. Komatik heavily loaded, with five skinned seals lashed behind for dog feed, sad eyed and obscenely nude, dripping fat and blood as we jolted through the soaking snow. Made 18 slow miles, camped in a tiny one room Eskimo house, very crowded. No one spoke English, I speak no Eskimo, we got along fine.

February 10. Horrible going. Reached Kamarsuk at noon, saw some patients, on to Boat Harbour which we reached in pitch dark very tired, several patients here. Very tired.

February 11. Dull morning, weather must improve sometime, off early, pushed all day, made Davis Inlet in snow and rain after dark, stayed with old friend Max Budgell, Indian Agent at this post, next day a blizzard, can't move.

February 13. Bright and clear, for a wonder, but going atrocious, edged along laboriously. Two teams in company now, Eskimos going to Kaipokok, we crossed one very long difficult portage across small mountain, reached Big Bay at dusk, comfortable night, no work.

February 1. Going not bad at first, but light shell of ice over snow cut dogs up badly, we leave bloody paw prints in snow for miles of painful travel. Poor dogs! Later going better, we reached Hopedale. With Reverend Fred Grubb as master of ceremonies we repeated the Nain clinic on slightly smaller scale. Some good cases. More toxoiding. Fred is doing this himself. Excellent.

February 15. Off for Kaipokok, a long narrow bay 35 miles long. Passed Ugjoktok Bay, reached small place where woman is dying of tuberculosis, had to break news to husband, we push on to Island Harbour. Guests of Jimmy McNeill overnight, a loyal friend of the Mission.

February 16. Up Kaipokok today. Awful going, dogs cut further, most of time walking or on snowshoes, my drivers earning their pay. One is jolly little round man, all muscles, springy as rubber ball, tireless and cheerful worker. Other is tall and lanky, likewise strong as a bull but considers himself the executive. Not unwilling to work when Henoch needs help though, and fine worker when he feels the time has come.

Dogs very tired, we cannot ride. Kaipokok seemed endless, snow got deeper and deeper near head of bay but long after dark we see the first lights of Three Rapids. Ended on snowshoes, dogs utterly spent, delighted to see the Grieves brothers again, who are running the pulpwood enterprise here. They have done a fine job of housing and care for the people, have fought against great odds including supply shortage, destruction of stores by fire, a local famine from failure of the seal fishery etc. Many ill patients here, Walter Grieve acting as assistant doctor, a long and busy clinic. He could stand and work for hours without fatigue. Some very ill or dying.

February 19. Poor going, snowing, went down bay as far as village called The Post, a Pentecostal Mission station. Gillett, the minister, very hospitable, consider he has done much for his tiny flock, teaching them boat building, running a community sawmill etc. Number of cases here, one dying of tuberculosis, several have recently recovered from diphtheria, one has a diphtheria heart.

February 20. Interminable trip down Kaipokok, bad going, rain and snow squalls all day, arrived at Makkovik late. Sudden drop down a very steep bank about two hundred feet high caught drivers unaware, we went down like a rocket, shearing small trees like matches, leaving trail of snowshoes, mitts, kettles etc. Drivers thought this screamingly funny, rolled in snow with merriment. Always jolly. Mr. George Harp, as usual soul of cheerfulness, like all Moravians very kind host. Very vigorous personality, some very advanced ideas and progressive outlook. Like him immensely, as do all of them. Busy clinic with his help for two days.

Many tuberculosis patients here. One dying. Has recently been diphtheria epidemic. Daily I am seeing signs of recent diphtheria. Have reason to believe I will find it active further south. Number of people have died of it between Nain and here, others dying now to south.

February 22. Goodbye to the Eskimos, very nice lads. New driver is Jim Andersen, fine big team, Jim is a very enterprising young Labradorman, small sawmill etc., good type. Two other boys with us, owners of some of the dogs, wish to make the trip. Pleasant party, started off in mild weather, sticky going. Shoot couple partridges. Managed to get to Harry Andersen's at Adlavik, stopping one house on the way. Three families here, number of patients amongst them, one woman for operation. Filthy weather the next day, hung up.

February 24. Off for Tishialuk, near Cape Harrison, where there is small American base. Going very poor, team is a fine big powerful one, large healthy dogs. Bays all ripped open by recent storms, ice either missing or unsafe. Crossed on loose slob ice around Salmon Cove Head, very unsteady feeling to see the pans lurch and sag under us, my driver knows what he is about. Made the American base just at twilight.

February 25 and 26. Blizzard, heavy snow, wild weather. Fed up. Entertained very kindly by my American hosts. Went to bed at midnight. At 3 a.m. Jim—sharing the dispensary with me—awoke, smelling smoke. Found kitchen full of smoke, red glow about range stovepipe. Called me. I found heavy smoke, kitchen untenable. Awoke the Americans, we got fire extinguishers. Smoke suffocating. My two boys partly overcome, were sleeping in kitchen, failed to awake. Recovered quickly outdoors.

Wind over 60 miles an hour, smothering drift, three feet of soft snow outside. Went back to help fight fire, on way saw that the whole peak of kitchen wing was afire inside. Advised Americans useless to to try to fight fire further. Commanding officer reached same conclusion. Got most of my gear out. Helped Americans in dwelling wing, rescuing all warm clothing we could find.

My own travelling gear in commanding officer's cabin, had hard time getting it, partly overcome, cut my head going through window which I had failed to open. Much blood, but only superficial, made me look startling in the firelight. Found that boys had failed to locate our big komatik box with much of our gear. Tried to get in kitchen to find it, building well aflame, burning embers falling. Opening doors, the gale blew in, scattered the flames, was able to search room in comparative comfort except for falling embers. Found box under pile of greatcoats, rescued these as well as box—they came in handy.

Building all aflame, except dispensary, which I managed to enter, rescued two sacks instruments and drugs, as feared might have burns or injuries to treat. Within 25 minutes of start building was one vast bed of embers, erupting bursts of flame from one end where large oil storage tank had been. Half dressed, up to waist in snow, in the blizzard, many small burns but no serious injury and feeling fine. What next?

Found a nearby shed, stored all our gear, secured our dogs. Found a nearby Quonset hut inhabited by the local caretaker, we all joined forces and went there, Mrs. Dickers got some coffee and food. Rested two hours. Went over to Tishialuk, two miles away, still blowing hard and drifting, going very difficult. Cleaned up. Large dental clinic, number of general patients.

February 28. Drifting wildly, but possible to travel after noon. Went to Tilt Cove, up small mountain, new deep snow, foul going, mostly snowshoes. Snowshoes are the bane of winter travel. Wet clinging snow towards the latter part of the afternoon, every step one lifts pounds of snow. The tips catch in the deep snow, trip me at every step. Dogs keep overtaking me, must run much of time. Wonder why I ever chose Labrador for a life work. At Tilt Cove tragically poor little house, leaky roof, nothing to eat! The master of the house arrives soon after with barrel of flour. Two Eskimo women have been hungry during the storm.

February 29. Off for Wolfrey's Cove via Bob's Brook. A single family at each, very lonely. Stay at Wolfrey's Cove for night.

March 1. The long portage from the sea to Pottle's Bay, across the Big Neck—a fine place to get lost on, few landmarks, only one small belt of woods at Halfway Brook. Going poor, but we manage to cross in one day, reach Pottle's Bay at dusk. No one there, three empty houses, a note on one "Sick. Gone to Rocky Cove." House locked but the thoughtful owner left porch open, with stove set up in it with firewood and cooking utensils available. It is a kind country. Good night and comfortable rest.

March 2. Hope I shall meet my Cartwright team today. Had expected to meet it at Pottle's Bay. Stop at Rocky Cove, many patients, toxoid for children, a long busy clinic. One hopeless cancer, a tuberculosis, one or two other things. On to Fox Cove. Meet my team on way, with John Dyson of Batteau my driver. Transfer some of my baggage, the two teams proceed to Ticoralak for the night. On to Rigolet, arriving at noon. Here I part with Jim Andersen and leave, after a brisk clinic in the village and a comfortable night as guest of the hospitable Hudson bay post manager, Sam Dawe. Jack Watts, Mission superintendent, North West River station down here to meet me, mail and all the news. Good to see him again, I give him mail to go via Goose Bay.

March 4. Off up Double Mer to Pompey's Head. Double Mer a long narrow cul-de-sac 40 miles long, runs off of Hamilton Inlet and parallel to it. Night at Pompey's Head. Send another patient from here to North West River for hospitalization—that makes four since Rocky Cove.

March 5. Miserable going, cross a 10 mile portage to

Hamilton Inlet, it is too dark and too late to risk the bad ice across to Peter Lewis Brook, whence one goes down Back Bay, the ice is very bad from the mild weather, one team went through last week. We follow the shore instead, making for Carawalla Head where there is a family of Eskimos. Neither of us has ever been there, it is pitch dark. Our lead dog loses the trail, is checked just before we go off the ice into open water. We deduce we must be near Carawalla—we are, thank heavens. Exhausted, dogs even more so. Jolly Eskimo family, most hospitable. Long dental clinic, other odd jobs, then bed.

March 6. Filthy day, snowing, thick. Charley Ikey knows how desperately worried I am about my patients at Cartwright, and all this delay. Should have been at Cartwright ten days ago. He volunteers to pilot us across the bad ice. Off in warm wet snow. Very thick. Charley flits ahead on snowshoes, the dogs trot most of the way but never catch him. Seven miles. Arriving at Peter Lewis Brook, Charley is not even breathing hard. Amazing, I think. I could have done it—have been doing so for weeks, but would be purple in the face, dizzy, and fatigued. More patients, we then take a pilot team because of the dangerous ice and leave for Pease Cove, camping for the night in the same shack we lunched in in December. John is sick, seems to have bronchitis. Both very tired. Our pilot agrees to take us on the next day as far as Ikey's Point. We take some of the dog's seal meat and cook it—one misses fresh meat terribly.

March 7. John quite sick. Stop at Ikey's Point for the night, although we reach there by noon, as John's condition worries me. Coughing heavily, feverish. Rest up, he seems better in morning, we start.

March 8. Down Back Bay, shell on the snow cuts the dogs feet cruelly, and we leave bloody flecks in the snow for miles. Poor dogs, tired and foot sore. Across the neck and down Flatwater Brook to Flatwater by dusk.

March 9. Off for Cartwright, but so many houses to visit and so much work to do only manage North River. The going started fairly good, but soon melted, then began to snow, then intermittent rain. Horrible day, tired at North River. Fell asleep quickly.

March 10. Bright sparkling morning, very cold, going is wonderful. Reach Cartwright in hour and a half, a trip which cost me a long weary day in Dec. Out of almost six weeks only one nice day, and only two hours of good going. Rain or snow all the rest of the time. Patients seen—324. Sent or advised to hospital—15, dental extractions—150, toxoid for diphtheria—134. Also, using only the subjective method I managed to provide eyeglasses for many people, most of them simple presbyopias who could no longer do near work like sewing without the help of glasses. Glad to get into a hot bath, and have a long soak before lying down on a real bed. Sunny day. All well at the station, thanks to a good staff.

Space forbids me to describe the southern trip, which soon followed. It took about a month, and took me to St. Mary's River in the Straits of Belle Isle. I saw almost exactly the same number of patients as north—323. The trip was not outstanding in any way, and going conditions were much better than those of the northern trip, as is usually the case in spring. Averaged more like 50 miles a day than the average of 25. Some bad ice. I did not go through. My driver was a seasoned pilot, but got a severe case of snowblindness on trip and was nearly completely blind, which complicated the navigation.

Diphtheria appeared but not badly and our chief trouble came from a flu epidemic which laid many villages low. On our return many houses were too sick to provide firewood and drinking water for themselves. A number of deaths, but in Sandwich Bay there were none at all except two or three in a tiny religious colony which has conscientious objections to medical care.

I did not get flu myself. My driver did, and bronchopneumonia with it, and I left him at his home on the way north, finishing the trip with a son of my old friend John Dyson. Hated to leave John Morris, my original southern driver, sick and miserable, but there was nothing else I could do. He recovered later. In the last week of April I went to North West River by dog team and there my travels were over. Almost—I had to go to Goose Bay, whence I flew to Montreal and St. John's Newfoundland and back to Goose, and that whole trip of two thousand miles took only 10 days. It had taken me 4 months of hard work to do 1700 miles by dog team.

It was a bad winter because of bad weather, but otherwise all went well and nothing untoward happened, and I ended up very fit indeed. The travelling is a slow and laborious job, and a lot of time is wasted, but there is no other way to cover the coast properly as of yet. Perhaps air travel will simplify things in the future. In the meantime I think I am quite capable of sticking at it for a few years yet. The hospital ship work of the summer is immensely pleasanter and quicker and more efficient, but Labrador is Labrador.

WINTER MEDICAL PATROL, 1947-48

The wind ridges of snow on the bay ice were white and pale gold in the clarity of morning light, with sharp-cut shadows of violet. During the night the razor wind had carved and streamlined them till they were a little too hard and a little too high for the frailty of skis and landing gear, and they stretched endlessly like motionless waves on the level ice. The aircraft came at the appointed time, though, and circled brilliant yellow against the pale blue, and we knew he would attempt to land. Then the long wail of wings, a descending note in the frosty wind, and he was on the ice and lurching awkwardly across the windrows, a huge and unseasonable butterfly, to the bay shore.

Each year the Royal Canadian Air Force flies me north on the first stage of my northern winter trip. By this means long weeks of hard travelling are eliminated, and I can start fresh at Nain. My plan for this year was a departure, since I proposed to fly to Nain, pick up a team and proceed on north, beyond the range of this aircraft, to Hebron. I would call at every settlement and home from this place south, returning at last to North West River again. The trip, counting all detours up bays or around bad ice, would be just under a thousand miles. The assistance of the Royal Canadian Air Force would mean the visiting of hundreds of people who would otherwise have had to wait a full twelve months between summer seasons for a doctor's visit. The flight was one of those authorized by the Royal Canadian Air Force "in the interests of the public welfare." The public welfare of Labrador has been a matter of generous consideration by the Royal Canadian Air Force ever since the establishment of Goose Bay.

Flight Lieutenant Barney Hartman was pilot of the Norseman, and waved from the window as the aircraft stopped. Expert on northern flying and the North, Barney is likewise friend to everyone in it. When the wings of the Royal Canadian Air Force are summoned in emergency or disaster, or to the relief of the injured or critically ill, it is Barney who answers the call. Often he has collaborated with the Grenfell Mission or come to our aid when aid was needful, and today he makes this flight in the interests of several hundred Eskimos far to the north.

My medical supplies and travelling kit, a pile of food cases, guns, snowshoes, clothing and medical cases, were already piled out on the ice, and we load the plane at once, for our weather report puts a limit on the duration of the good weather and we are in a hurry. The plane is unexpectedly warm after the piercing wind on the bay ice, made colder yet in the icy slip-stream of the propellor. Then the slow staggering progress across the hard drifts out onto the open ice, and the sudden shocking bellow of power, swelling to a sustained thunder almost obscene in the northern stillness. The aircraft presses forward eagerly, sledge blows strike upward through the slender landing gear, and I watch with wonder the ski below me slammed and battered by hard drift. Then the sickening lurches and the savage pounding fade, and the Norseman swings exultantly up into the cold peace of the sky. "That ice," observes Barney thoughtfully, "is really rugged this morning."

North West River falls away below us, looking surprisingly small and bleak from the air, and we fly parallel with Grand Lake for a time, a sheet of black ice veined with white snow-ridges, and then in across country. Snow-covered forest begins to yield to lean scrub along the watercourses and the woods thin to fringes and strips in sheltered places. The land climbs ever, and rocky outcrops thrust up through the snow, then come the mountains terrible in desolation, and now again we reach salt water, with chains of black rocky islets brooding over shifting sea ice, which reaches eastward into infinity. The hills become frowning black and savagely forbidding. Surely no life can survive in such a world.

Here below us, though, are the tiny blocks of Nain village. Sudden silence and the long whistling descent, and we hang suspended above the racing ice a moment before the bunt and soft tremble of skis tells us we are down. Around the plane crowds all of Nain, round-faced button-eyed little children, jolly bandylegged hunters, the laughing girls, the whole village bubbles with fun. The Reverend Bill Peacock, Moravian Mission Superintendent, and his staff are here too, and I am glad to go again into his hospitable home, which will be my headquarters for a while.

Five days are well spent in Nain, patients almost steadily from dawn to dark hours, while Bill interprets and helps without break, and we do minor operations, examinations, treatments, and arrange for the disposition of certain cases. Bill arranges a team for Hebron, and I sort out my equipment, some of which will be cached at Nain. Without benefit of the profound experience and knowledge of the Moravians and their constant material and moral help, I would be unable to do anything here. This help is given gladly and freely, as usual.

We leave Nain on a dull morning, moderately cold. Two Eskimo drivers on this team, neither speaks any English. Fourteen dogs, none too many for our load, require much attention. Drivers are cheery and competent looking, are to prove the kindest and most considerate of companions. The trip is to take us across the jagged and desolate Kiglapait Mountains, a trail on which there are no houses or shelters for a weary distance, and the climb up into the hills is formidable. We climb most of the day, winding for miles up a stream-bed and later up rolling hills. Often we must haul on the traces with the dogs to drag the heavily loaded komatik up the steep slope, and it gives you some insight into the dog's point of view. I am flabby and in poor condition after five weeks' recent trip in the States and Canada, and my drivers, who can run cheerfully up a half mile of steep hillside are amused at my fatigue. I determine I shall keep up, and hope my coronary system is in good condition.

The exertion is acutely painful, and the going is very bad. The dogs tire, and the komatik grinds slowly through dry snow, and at dusk we have come less than forty-five miles. We plod on three hours after dark and give it up, making camp in a snow house or igloo. Intensely cold up here in the hills, and it seems colder inside than out. Our primus stove works badly, and we make a cold supper of it, everything frozen stiff and the damp new bread I brought harder than concrete, yielding finally to a sharp axe. The cold must be felt to be appreciated. The sky is a brilliant blue-black, with enormous stars and a pale mist of northern lights, and the frost cuts at my lungs as I take a last look before turning in.

Even under my sleeping bag my sealskin boots are frozen like sheet-steel in the morning, must be thawed out under my clothes. Breakfast, too, is frozen solid except in a few spots where it is burnt, but the tea is plentiful and scalding. Just before dawn we leave the igloo behind us, a tiny lonely hummock in the vastness of the hills. Just ahead of us are the slender spires of the Kiglapait peaks, soaring unbelievably above us. Hour after hour we work amongst them, endlessly up and then down, and the dry snow is no more slippery than so much sand. At last we drop off the edge of the world, and begin the long descent, and at noon we are again on saltwater ice, and so to Udlik. Here Joe Millik urges me to stay, and we promise to spend a night on the way back. Ten or twelve miles of ice, with one preposterously steep hill at the end, and we reach the lonely Nutak trading post just before dark. Here there is a good deal of work to be done, and since the next day is one of furiously drifting snow and high winds, I stay over, leaving the following morning in company with the team of the Newfoundland Ranger who is bound north also. At noon we camp together and lunch out of his grub box, sumptuous compared to the dehydrated and concentrated atrocities I must carry if my food is to last me nearly a thousand miles.

All day we toil up steep slopes and then, like thunderbolts, go roaring down the other side. At dark we are still a long way from Green Cove, and it begins to snow a light feathery powder. The scene is gloomily magnificent with enormous cliffs looming through the snow flurries three thousand feet above us, and the sombreness of the gathering night is almost frightening. A long time later, though, a spark winks out of the dark, and we come to Green Cove, Eskimo hamlet of three families. My host has chronic far advanced pulmonary tuberculosis of both lungs, and since the visit of last summer in *Maraval* has developed what seems to be tuberculosis of the spine. He was a great hunter and a strong man and resents dying young, but is very thoughtful as a host.

Off at sun-up, on a powder of new snow. Hebron is not far, and at noon the houses come into sight, this last settlement on the road north. There is no longer any post on the Labrador north of Hebron Bay, and I think as I feel the deathly cold draft coming off the hills that it is just as well. The entire population comes running out to welcome us, and make up by their warmth the deficiencies of the climate. Fred and Marjorie Grubb are in the forefront, and take me to their quarters in the Moravian building. After a magnificent dinner we go to work.

There is no fuel in Hebron this winter. The schooner that was to bring it failed to come, and the people are burning handfuls of willow and bits of seal fat. This is tragic, as the seal oil commands excellent prices this year, and some families have burnt over two hundred dollars worth already. The stench of this type of fire reminds one of a martyrdom by fire, and kettles refuse to boil over the smoky flame. Everyone seems to have skin disease, which they attribute to the difficulty of getting water to wash with, and a tragic number of children have corneal ulcers which will prevent them from ever being great hunters or needlewomen. Blindness is all too common amongst the Eskimos.

Fred works with me tirelessly. In three or four days, all is done, and I am ready to start south, but furious drift holds me back one day. A fair number of operations are done, none of them very major, and a great number of teeth extracted. Notes are made for a possible X-ray survey next summer, and all in all the visit is worthwhile. We leave on March 16, in early afternoon, snow drifting hard but the weather bright and clear. I must keep working on my face to prevent freezing, but the going is good and we climb the hills easily. Green Cove this night, and on south next morning, passing inside the looming majesty of Cape Mugford, whose high battlements frown down on us while we are still thirty miles away. We reach the solitary house at Parkaivik during the twilight, and go in for the night. No one speaks a word of English, my Eskimo is hopeless, but we have a cheery evening, and the floor is nicely level when I turn in. Lumps or loose boards in Labrador floors are the bane of one's existence, as they have a remarkable ability to pick out bony prominences and convert them into bony concavities, and holes in the floor are worse again.

We reach Nutak about noon of the 18th, and I lunch with the genial Max Budgell, who seems to revel in the utter isolation of this outpost. This night with Joe Millik in Udlik, where I have the unheard-of luxury of a room to myself and a sofa to sleep on. Floors are not bad, but there is nothing like a table or sofa to spread one's sleeping bag on, and it is much warmer, and tonight I am as comfortable as if sleeping in a bed.

We leave at daybreak, determined to get all the way to Nain in one long leg, over seventy miles, and the trip up into the mountains seems interminable. I am not feeling well and wish the day were done. It drifts hard, and the drift swirls out of the passes like driven smoke, or hangs in lacy fringes around the mountain peaks. Fourteen hours across the Kiglapaits, stopping once for a frost-bitten lunch, and we drop down through the dusk along an icy brook. Once we lose control and skid sideways down the ravine and over a frozen waterfall, to the vast amusement of myself and one of the drivers. The other one is slower to laugh, having gone over the waterfall in a sitting position.

At dark we take the ice of Nain Bay, and I realize that I am bitterly cold, colder than I have ever been, and wretchedly stiff. I must run to keep from freezing, and my sickness makes running very unpleasant. The drift swirls out of the dark with a personal malevolence. I stumble on patches of slippery ice or plow through drifts and count my steps endlessly with a mind too numb to do anything else. The bay stretches endlessly, and once when we climb across a rocky island and I think we are about to reach Nain, the bay opens again and I realize it is still many miles, and could almost weep with cold and fatigue. The Eskimos are not enjoying it either, but are making an effort to be cheerful and lively, and are concerned about my illness. I remember that Sem is twenty years older than I am and has arthritis and has been running almost all day so that I may ride when I wish, and realize that I should be ashamed of myself. The cold creeps in, but I reject it fiercely and run for a long stretch, and Paul's Island looks a little nearer, and at last a spark winks under the hills and then glows warm, and the dogs pick up their tails and trot, and I reflect that there is no such thing as a trail with no end. The trick is getting there.

At Nain, Bill thaws me out with a boiler of hot soup. Eighteen hours is too much of a day's run, and I remember longingly a winter spent on a minesweeper in the tropics. A real bed, with sheets, and never a dream. Two days are required to make ready, but we leave on the 20th, with a fresh team. The drivers must miss the Easter Festival, the big event of the year, but they know I am needed south and come cheerfully enough. They will be paid about four dollars a day for a week of a hundred hours on the average, and must supply their own dog feed, which will cut deep into the profits.

We leave in the afternoon, for a short run to Voisey's Bay. Here lies Amos Voisey, dying of inoperable cancer of the mouth and starving because he cannot eat. "Is there any hope, doctor? Should I get a team and go south?" I tell him there is none at all.

He chuckles feebly. "It's not the thought of dying that frightened me, you know. It was the thought of that trip south in this condition. If you say I can't help my family by going south, I'm content to die in this house I built myself. You'll stay and yarn with me tonight. It'll be my last yarn about old times." Morphine and codeine, all I have, but enough for his last days. Soon he is free of pain and quite cheerful. For hours he talks, pouring forth his experience, his ideas about the country and its problems, what he thinks the people can do to make best use of the country's resources. I am fascinated and go to sleep only at his insistence, only an hour or two before starting time.

Next afternoon we reach Boat Harbour in a blinding snow flurry, and break into the big empty home of Chesley Ford, passing a comfortable night on the kitchen floor of this fine house. We leave at dawn in hard drift, and the flying snow boils out of the mountain gaps like a smoke screen. The surface of the snow smokes and shifts as one watches it, and drift finds its way into the tiniest opening in clothing. Up into Shango Bay on a wild goose chase after a supposed diphtheria, and then on to Davis Inlet, which we reach at four o'clock. Drifting violently, but sunny. The post is utterly deserted and locked up, so we push on down the inlet and up into Flowers Bay for the night. None of us have ever been there, and we know only vaguely where the house is. We take the wrong side of the bay in the dark, and through ten miles of hummocks and "ballicatters," great frozen rosettes of ice over boulders in the shallow water below. Scrambling and stumbling through these in the flying drift, unhooking fouled dog traces or splicing a broken one, we pray that we will not break a runner of the wildly slamming komatik. At 11 o'clock we see the lights—which we almost pass in the drift—and soon we are in shelter.

The next day across the long portage to Big Bay, and by twilight into Hopedale. Here again the friendly Moravian station and Mr. Grubb, senior, for several days of medical aid. We leave after lunch on March 27, a warm sultry day without a breath of wind. We must cross a big bay, going well out to sea, and I am not familiar with the road. An hour later there is a draft of southeasterly wind, steadying to a breeze and within a half hour becoming a screaming white fury. Islands, landmarks, everything is blotted out, and we can barely see our dogs. We try to follow the trail of a team just ahead of us, but our lead dog will not face the wind and cannot follow the trail, and so one of us must run to either side looking for a runner mark here, a dog-track uncovered by the wind there, scanty evidence that we are still on the track. We hope the team ahead knows what he is about, for conditions are bad. I freeze my face considerably but am too busy to care—now. Looking to windward is impossible, and the drift is suffocating. The dogs are almost unmanageable. We learn later that someone froze to death near Hopedale this afternoon, much damage is done southward. Five hours of this is quite enough, and we can only guess at our position.

Once we catch a glimpse of a rocky islet, probably one of those outside of Tikkeratsuk, where we hope to take shelter. The nature of the ice changes and we guess we are nearing land. We have lost the other team's trail by now, but soon we see low land through the drift, and a few bushes, and we cross high tidal ballicaters and there again is the trail we were following before. Reassured, we cross a neck and again come out on ice, hummocky and tidal, and conclude we must be in a tidal inlet. The drift screams down the shore, and we creep through the hummocks, perhaps 20 yards from the shore line, for what seems an interminable length of time. One of my drivers runs ashore and climbs a bank, where he stands motionless for perhaps five minutes. The flying scud lightens a moment and he points, and we see a building dimly, perhaps forty yards from us. It is a fish stage, and the house must be nearby. At length we find the house, another thirty yards further, and in front of it are two other teams unharnessing. They too have been driven in, arriving just ahead of us. The house is deserted, but we break into it cheerfully and help each other unharness and unload, and all gear is carried inside. The wretched dogs huddle in the porch, eyes gummed with ice, and a thick powdering of fine snow settles over them, burying them completely. There is no firewood, but we demolish a small outhouse and start a fire. The stovepipe had collapsed, but we repair it with bits of tin can, and in an hour all is snug and warm and candles glow in the dark.

The building trembles sometimes, but we are preoccupied with an enormous stew, to which everyone contributes something, and the difficulties of the day dissolve into repletion and rest, good tobacco smoke, and tales of other storms. Mike Solomon, my Eskimo driver, tries out some English. "Bad outside tonight, snow put out pipes I s'pose. More good in house." I think, as I go to sleep, that the occupant of the Royal Suite at the Waldorf Astoria is tonight less contented than am I, and when snow drifts down on my face through the stove-pipe opening, I pull the eider-down sleeping bag across my face and wonder at its softness and warmth. Even the floor seems soft.

Next morning a rough cold run to Island Harbour, where there is a good deal of medical work, and I rest the remainder of the day. My face is bothering me, and my drivers have frozen theirs slightly, and we are sick of the wretched endless drifting snow. After a few weeks it becomes utterly hateful, chilling one down, filtering into one's clothing to melt and freeze, and of course it is the worst cause of frostbite. It takes the joy out of eating on the trail. The Labrador men take it in strides but love it not.

Up Kaipokok on the 28th, to Postville, the little Pentecostal community, where the hospitality is up to the best of Labrador standards. Here is much tuberculosis and human tragedy, and the recent collapse of the pulp-cutting enterprise at Three Rapids has left everyone hungry and discouraged. We talk about the Cooperative movement, which the people are considering undertaking. Thence the following day to Makkovik, where the Moravian post was lately destroyed by fire. We eat at dusk, just before entering the village, which we know is just above the starvation level.

Here the Reverend George Harp is quietly and cheerfully rebuilding the physical destruction of a generation's labour—with broken tools and little in the way of resources but courage. They have moved into an old storehouse, having saved nothing from the fire, and have set up housekeeping as if nothing had happened. I attend service in the little temporary church, and the message is one of cheer and strength. Two days here. The Harps are full of fun, and eager for open water and building supplies. A number of patients, none very sick.

I leave with a new team for Tishialuk, where Sam Broomfield from North West River is to take me home, and reach the American base and radio station on the second day. Here, a year ago, I nearly lost my life when the building caught fire at 2 a.m. during a blizzard, and we escaped with some difficulty, two of my party being overcome for a time by smoke. We had ended up out in the storm, watching our shelter explode in bursts of blazing oil and crashing rafters. Unpleasant enough for me, it must have been hideous for the American soldiers, recently arrived by air from the States and utterly unused to the Labrador climate and country. The completely rebuilt station is a going concern again, and after a day of medical work and a night of pleasant hospitality, I meet Sam Broomfield on schedule and proceed south. We have four extra dogs which we are taking south to their owner at Goose Bay, beautiful animals, and our team is a powerful one.

Wolfrey's Cove the night of April 3, from where we will leave the sea and cut across the peninsula separating us from Hamilton Inlet. We spend the night in a tiny one-room house which is held up only by one big log and stands tottering on the lonely seashore. The two old people in this house have been starving too many years to mind it any more, the young man has never known anything better, and all in all it is a very happy home, albeit in need of soap for a number of years. Also Flit [insecticide]. No one could be kinder, though, and when we leave, we are presented with a beautiful fresh eider duck and a brace of white partridge, which they insist we take.

Now the long portage overland, rolling hill and tundra. There has been very little snow this year, and most of this has blown away. Today is warm, almost up to the freezing point. In sheltered places the snow melts fast, and there is much bare ground and raw rock to drag the unwilling komatik across. Sam is endlessly cheerful, kind, full of fun, and one of the most gifted of mimics. He is the best driver I have ever travelled with, and loves his dogs. He keeps them on the jump, too, and threatens them with dreadful things when they wander. The dogs have had a hard time. Their feet are badly cut, and the trail behind us is speckled with blood. We take two of them out of harness, and they trot alongside painfully.

Pottle's Bay in the afternoon, a branch of Hamilton Inlet, and I am barely a hundred and fifty miles from home. It is beginning to snow when we arrive. Both families here have had diphtheria recently and are recovering. They have the pharyngeal palsy that so often follows this disease and sound like a conclave of cleft palates, but are feeling better every day. Why none of them died remains a profound mystery. They urge us to hurry on to Bluff Head, where Joseph Rich is very ill. We press on another nine miles, well out of our way, and enter the house in time to watch his death. He has stopped breathing, but has some pulse for a few seconds. The family is huddled in the front room. Nine miles to a neighbour, 45 to a trading post, 150 to a hospital or even a minister to bury the body which in hospital would still be alive. Make a coffin out of scrap lumber, I advise, and pack the body in salt. It can be buried this spring, when the ground thaws out.

We proceed to Rocky Cove, which is reached an hour after dark. A magnificent day's run, spoiled only by the loss of a life that might have been saved had I wasted one less day along the way. During the afternoon the poor dogs have suffered greatly. Three of them are terribly lame now, and out of harness. I watch one, a great silky red animal who runs just off one quarter of the komatik. He cries with pain as he runs, and leaves pink stains in the snow, and the one shoulder is sprained, but the long-legged even lope goes smoothly on, mile after mile. Sometimes his foot sinks into the snow or slips into a hole, and he cries out shrilly in pain, and Sam and I are helpless to do anything for him. He must follow if he can. Behind us hobbles another, magnificent in his pure white coat, suffering in silence. A dog has a hard life and rarely lives more than six or seven years. He has no certitude nor comfort from the time he leaves the warmth of his mother's body, but he is a happy-go-lucky creature with a sense of fun. Their civil wars are savage, their mating incredibly ferocious, but they are cheerful and loyal, and as friendly as any dogs anywhere, and they have the added dignity of being workers instead of companions or toys, and indeed they love their work and are happiest on the trail, and they are an important part of this hard but magnificent country.

April 5 we reach Double Mer, where warm weather and a slashing rain delay us for one day, which we spend with one Bill Wolfrey, a master of the Tall Story.

April 7 off to Rigolet, via a long detour up Double Mer to see a woman with advanced tuberculosis superimposed on pernicious anemia. Not much to offer in encouragement. Crossing the neck of land between Double Mer Inlet and the Narrows, about five miles took four hours. Wet, sticky snow, we go through to our waists. The komatik runs a few yards and then runs off the melting remnants of the trail and buries its nose in wet snow. Laboriously dug out and put on the road, it runs a few yards again, we are wringing with exertion, and the woods seem endless. Lunch with Mr. Dawe of the Hudson Bay Company, a few patients to see, and we press on up the Narrows, hugging the rim of shore ice.

On one side the vertical hillside, on the other the black racing water of the Narrows, our path is a narrow highway of irregular and very slippery ice which slopes to the water, and Sam keeps us on course with considerable skill. The last time I came here my driver had just reassured me that practically no one ever fell in when there was a scream for help from the team behind us, and we were half an hour pulling them out of the icy Narrows. Most of their load was lost. No accidents this time, and we camp in a tiny house at Mulliauk Cove, leaving the next morning.

The going is excellent, and we check off mile after smooth mile. Something I ate has proven a bad investment, and I am compelled to cancel several visits and make haste for Valley's Bight, where I brood over unpleasant visions of trying to take out my own appendix under local, and try to cheer up my host who is going through an even worse time of it with sciatica. Codeine for supper, both of us, and both of us feel stiff and sore but reasonably improved in the morning, and we press on, reaching the home of my brother at Salt Water Pond, only 14 miles from home. I would have done better, but like a fool went through the ice, or rather the komatik went through the ice and I went in trying to pull it out of the water. Up to my shoulders only—one never feels so wet if one's hair remains dry—but the water was cool. I must strip and change out there on the bay in the wind, and find the wind less mild than I had previously thought.

Leave my brother Harry's in morning, back-tracking to Mulligan to do a medical round, calling at

North West Islands. Real Labradormen here, of dignity and education, comparatively prosperous as the result of thrift and hard, skillful labour. Full of fun, charming hosts, they make the day pass quickly, and back to Harry's at night, where I run over to people in Salt Pond who wish to see the doctor. In the morning we leave at a sensible hour, for I am weary of getting up before daylight, and my sister-in-law Peggy does not awaken me. Fresh eggs for breakfast, and all sorts of luxuries I have not seen for weeks. North West River for dinner, and then to work on my patients with Margaret Ormerod, my nurse in charge.

The trip is over, just under six weeks. This may not sound much to some of you, who may think a winter trip should last all winter. There were, and before breakup must still be, other trips, but the long one, the one I look forward to with most misgivings, is over, and I am back sound, and none of my patients have died in my absence.

WINTER MEDICAL PATROL, 1948-49

[To Dr. Curtis]

There is not a great deal of interest to report to you. I completed a medical trip from Saglek Fjord to North West River in just about six weeks, phenomenally rotten going the whole way and the worst trip I have ever made, but the travelling conditions in general have not been up to the average standard this winter. I don't know the statistics on the trip yet, but I think we saw about 450 patients.

You may have heard reports of influenza at Hebron, which broke out just after I left and resulted in a mercy flight and much excitement. It was a mild disease, and there were no deaths. I went through the whole business at Nain, every single Eskimo having it while I was there, and there were only two whose survival seemed doubtful at any time. They both looked as if they might recover when I left.

The trip from Hebron north to Saglek and back is a picturesque one in what is probably the most primitive part of the entire country. We used snow houses regularly except for one night in a sod house, half underground and only about 3 feet high, occupied by two families. I saw in this house the only stone seal-oil lamp I have ever seen in service, and I must say they make a lovely light and no smell. They make a good deal of heat. At this house, too, we had "Kuak," frozen raw seal meat, for supper. Please don't regard this as a hardship. I had lots of frozen beans in my grub box but ate raw seal because it was served to me. It's not bad, either.

We had either dry winter-type going all the way south, or new deep snow. I crossed from Napaktok to Okak Bay on snowshoes. That is the high pass known as Itiblisoak, inside of Cape Mugford, and I found it quite a climb. I guess I am getting old. In general there was a good deal of foot work connected with the trip. I got flu at Nain and had that for the next 250 miles. It didn't matter; everyone else had had it or was having it, but that made travelling additionally strenuous. South of Cape Harrison we struck plenty of fresh meat, killing twenty white partridge, four eider duck and two seals in quick succession, and felt fine immediately. A lack of fresh meat can be a real problem in this country, and one can tell the difference, subjectively, very quickly after getting meat. There is a prompt increase of endurance and a feeling of well-being which you cannot get on bread and tea or dehydrated soups and the like.

Surgery was confined to minor procedures, and I struck no real surgical emergencies. I found a fair number of cases for Cartwright and St. Anthony in the way of elective operations for summer. I am getting to know the people north better all the time and to win their confidence. Tuberculosis is fairly common, and I saw a good many clinically far advanced cases tottering through their last months. There were seven or eight deaths from this disease in Nain and Hebron alone since the last visit of the *Maraval*, and more to come. The people are showing a willingness to accept treatment, however, which they never did before, and I picked up one or two favourable cases as usual, which are now in hospital.

All in all, my chief points would be the prevalence of tuberculosis and the truly shocking amount of eye infections with the number of people in the various stages from early "kallak" to full blindness. These are mostly from Hopedale northwards. Malnutrition is the only other widespread disease at present, and a number of babies were lost through lack of milk. I am trying to arrange with Government now to set up depots of powdered milk for the northern communities, to prevent the needless deaths of infants in the future. There are three babies in Hebron district and Okak whose mothers died of tuberculosis this winter and who are now actually starving, nothing to feed them but flour—not a balanced diet for an infant under six months. Health otherwise was good, and there were not many acutely ill. I don't know what sequelae will follow in the train of the flu, but would expect the usual flare-up of tuberculosis. The Moravians were the spirit of kindness and cooperation, as was everyone. The trip was physically more difficult than usual, as a result of poor travelling conditions, but was otherwise uneventful and fairly routine.

WINTER MEDICAL PATROL, 1949-50

[To Dr. Curtis]

My trip north began, after a series of last-minute delays and minor emergencies, from Goose Bay in the Royal Canadian Air Force's Dakota aircraft. The weather was bright, clear, and cold. I remained at Hebron three days, working with the Reverend Grubb, senior, who helped me with interpreting and organization, and we saw a number of patients. One, whose X-ray you saw last autumn and whom you recommended for hospitalization, was sent back in the aircraft which brought me.

The seal fisheries were very poor last autumn, the result of premature freeze-up in the bays, and dog feed is desperately scarce throughout the country. The team I left with on the 23rd was thin and in poor condition, and the travelling conditions were poor, with dry going and hard hauling. I went to Napaktok the first day, to see an eye case, and thence on to Green Cove, arriving several hours after dark. I stayed in a house with a nearly moribund tuberculosis case, an old woman whose husband died of tuberculosis not long ago. She was alone in the house when I arrived, with a temperature of 104, and there was not even a fire in the stove. House was filthy dirty, which was no fault of our tragic hostess. Narcotics were all we could offer to relieve her distress, and we left at daylight the next day for Nutak. The going was abominable, and soon I took to snowshoes, going ahead. Crossed Itiblisoak, a very high and difficult portage with a climb I estimate at 1,200 feet of very steep gradient, and also the next portage overland, as I am getting to know the way fairly well now, going well ahead of the team for some hours. I was out of training and got tired, and my feet were cut up a bit by the slings, but anyway we made Nutak several hours after dark, very good considering the poor condition of the snow. I stayed until noon of the 26th, as there were a good many patients, and I arranged for evacuation by air of some of the worst but left the others, as I had no hospital accommodation at North West River for them, and they were cases I knew the Royal Canadian Air Force could not accept. I did one large and gory superficial operation, removing some very large keloids from the thorax of a man who was finding them a handicap in his work, Max Budgell, the government agent, acting as assistant. Saw about fifty patients here. Left noon on the 26th, starting with a very hard climb up the Nutak hills in poor going. I had engaged a new team here to take me to Hopedale, with two Eskimos, Zacharias Townley and Jonathan Kohlmeister, both of whom knew several words of English to supplement my meagre Eskimo.

Spent the night at Udlik, with Joe Millik, one of the most entertaining characters in the north, and was a success amongst the Eskimos there with some conjuring tricks. Quite a few cases of different types, and Joe, the perfect host, sacrificed two teeth to the cause of hospitality, to demonstrate his faith in me. Magic failed, I had to use instruments.

Left at dawn, atrocious going again. We never get

a break with travelling conditions. Took to snowshoes and walked the approaches to Korakulik and up the Kiglapait Mountains. Hard snowshoeing and the climb up the mountains seems interminable. It is said to be 2,500 feet, but it impresses me as nearer 3,000, although the charts give the elevation of this land at only 3,000, and of course we do not go quite to the top, taking a pass. This one always makes me wonder how my coronary circulation is.

Mostly on snowshoes today, up and down endless barren mountain tops and we begin the descent near dusk, picking up a brook which is icy and for the first time this trip we move fast—too fast in the dark, with the snow drifting before a rising wind. So we stopped on the first big snowdrift and the Eskimos built us a snowhouse, and glad I am to be in out of the cold and the fine driving little drift which seems never to stop in this country. Safely installed by ten o'clock, and eat well, sleeping fairly comfortably and leaving again at daylight. The dogs are underfed and thin and lack energy, so progress is painfully slow. Today I ride most of the time, and get astonishingly cold for this time of year, as it is drifting hard on the ice. Arrived at Nain pale blue and shivering, to the amusement of the Peacocks, who provide a vast hot meal and hot water for a real wash. In the north there is little fuel to spare for melting water and washing is at a premium in most of the homes and of course unthinkable in a snowhouse, where it would probably freeze up on you.

Very busy at Nain, a very large crowd being in for the Easter festivals, and clinics start at 8:30 am and run almost to midnight most days. Bill Peacock is tireless as interpreter and helper, and Mrs. Peacock keeps the instruments and equipment clean and doubles as nurse, and we finish in five fast days, during which we see about 150 cases and do a number of minor surgical procedures and incidentally over a hundred dental extractions. Again several patients evacuated by aircraft. We are finished with Nain on Sunday morning and leave immediately for Voisey's Bay, where the widow of old Amos Voisey holds gentle sway. The annual gift of a beautiful pair of skin boots, the perpetual legacy of old Amos to the Grenfell Doctor, whoever he may be.

I leave at daylight for Kamarsuk, where we see several patients and engage a pilot team to take some of the load. My drivers are not too sure of the road, and I find this terrain completely bewildering. We make the empty house at Boat Harbour just after dark, through the usual rotten going, and the dogs are very tired. Up at dawn on our way, the pilot team putting us on the road and leaving us. There is by now a good deal of daylight, and this dawn-to-dusk business is pretty strenuous, but going is so bad we must keep moving if we are ever to get anywhere. The dogs are very tired and are showing signs of failing. Little feed for them. We lose our track near Davis Inlet and follow a rather faint trail which we assume to be that of the mailman, who passed by two days ago. At dusk we pass into a long narrow cul-de-sac none of us have ever seen before, and it is beginning to snow. We hope we are not on the track of some casual deer hunter bound inland for the barrens, for we would never have dog feed to get us out again.

Soon it is pitch dark, so I get out a nearly exhausted flashlight and we go ahead of the dogs, as I have done most of the day, on snowshoes, searching for the now very faint track we are following. My inability to converse with my drivers does not make my days very sociable, and I am tired and irritable. The snowshoes seem to weigh a ton, and we have been going for 14 hours, and the track leads us into thick woods. Finally we come out on salt water ice again but have no idea where we are. It is now blowing and drifting as well as snowing and the track is hard to follow. We suspect we are about 20 miles from a house. The dogs are very tired and progress is slow.

Near midnight we reach Flowers Bay, and are glad to put up for the night. There is a bleeding placenta praevia here, so in the morning we leave early for Hopedale, the patient's husband driving her in a coach box. To lighten our wretched team I ride with him, having done over 30 miles on snowshoes the day before and beginning to feel it. His team is good, and despite snow and drift and poor visibility all day we reach Hopedale about two hours after dark. My team arrives about midnight in pitch dark and driving drift. The patient bled on the way, but not alarmingly, and I summon an aircraft, which turns up some days later and takes her to Goose.

Siegfried Hettasch and his wife are my hosts at Hopedale, and most considerate they are. Siegfried has considerable work of his own, as it is just before Easter and the church is busy, but he spends all his time with me, and we put in steady work without interruption for several days. On Good Friday the wind reaches 95 mph and the drift is indescribable, and I wonder what would be the fate of anyone caught out in it. I work fast and am remorseless with poor Siegfried, who is most helpful, and the work is done in time for me to leave for Island Harbour on April 7 with a new team, pitifully thin hungry little beasts who are well handled by Willie Winters.

You can only get so much work out of so much dog, and these little creatures shrink visibly with each mile, for again we have no decent dog feed. So slow is progress that we reach Tikkeratsuk too late to continue, and camp in an empty summer house, leaving at daylight. Island Harbour at noon, but alas, the expected dog feed is not available, and our dogs are unable to continue today. Willie is worried, for he suspects the run up Kaipokok Bay is going to be bad. We leave at daylight the next day from the hospitable Jimmie McNeill's, and a mile or two out I take to snowshoes and go on ahead. It begins to snow, and the going is terrible. It is even hard walking on snowshoes and gets worse, and I leave my team miles behind, which is a relief from watching the poor starved little things struggling in the soft snow. At noon I stop and wait, building a fire.

At last I hear my teamster urging the poor dogs, and at length they emerge from the little belt of woods ending the portage, and we boil up, eat and leave. I go ahead again. I am tired already, my feet are cut up and sore and I am dripping with perspiration and so hot that the snow melts on the scanty clothing I am wearing, making it uncomfortable. I have to stop twice and wait for the team, in order to bandage my feet, but am much relieved and can walk. I resort to my old habit of counting up to three thousand paces at a time and then stopping to see if I am any nearer the next point—visibly nearer, I mean. There is two feet of soft snow over an additional two feet of salt water and slush mixed on the ice, and the dogs are even more wretched than we are. Soaked with perspiration, and as the evening gets colder this starts to freeze in spots. Dripping wet and tired and sick of everything to do with Labrador. I am subject to a sort of acid indigestion, worse at times like this and worse in recent years, and it does little to make life pleasanter. Finally I count to two thousand paces at a time, sitting down to rest for three minutes at the end of each cycle, and by anaesthetizing my mind with numerals I seem to anaesthetize my feet and thighs too, but I cannot do more than two thousand at a time without having to stop.

I make Kaipokok at nearly nine, after over 40 miles of bad snowshoe walking no matter how you measure it. Too tired to take off snowshoes at first. Very stiff. By hurrying we get all the work done at this large and rapidly growing village the next day and leave early the following day. It is snowing heavily, and we can see nothing, but there is no wind, and I am in a hurry. Going is even worse, and we resort to snowshoes at once. A mile or two out the wind comes with a shriek and we are in a nice blizzard. The exhausted dogs can barely move, visibility is 50 yards and at times not ten. Every snowshoe step means lifting pounds of the stuff. Luckily I have a compass. We see little and must just keep on.

At noon we find a tiny cleft in one of the barren hills with a few stunted trees in it, and in this niche, near Iggiuk, we boil up. Shelter is fair, but snow drips into the chill meal we stuff down, and we are away again. Despite the snow, the spring sky is hard on the eyes, and we cannot wear snow goggles, as they ice up instantly. I feel incipient snow- blindness soon, and everything looks a curious green. Driving snow and icy particles cut conjunctivae painfully and sting our faces. My boots are sticky with blood. We have a small pilot team, and they are having a hard time. At dusk we manage to locate a certain abandoned house, but are quite a long time digging down to it, for it is quite buried in snow.

My three drivers are just as wretched, but they are solicitous for my comfort, whereas I am solicitous only for my own, and the realization makes me ashamed. And they are doing this work for a pittance, in order to help me bring what limited comfort I can to the sick, and I realize that self-pity is not a very durable consolation. Clearing out the kitchen we upset a bucket of rotten shark-liver oil and the filthy stuff seems the last and final straw. They howl with glee, and then patiently clean it all up and clear out the most comfortable part of the floor for my sleeping bag. One of them has no sleeping gear and refuses any of my stuff—not a bit cold, he explains, sleeping on the naked floor. They are full of praise for the miserable dehydrated and reconstituted military experiment I feed them for supper, along with a tin of sausage, and are indomitably cheerful. It is fun to have English-speaking drivers again, although no one could have been kinder or more considerate than the Eskimos I had from Hebron to Hopedale. So I do some conjuring tricks, and we all turn in feeling quite merry.

Next day is, if possible, worse than the last, but we are off again at first light, crossing the long portage to Makkovik Bay on snowshoes. The terrifying Ben's Cove slide, a very steep drop of 500 feet to Makkovik Bay, which has killed many dogs and broken up many komatiks and only this winter badly injured one driver, is today a morass of soft new snow, and we have to haul our load down a slope down which I shot like a runaway comet last year. Makkovik Bay is a smother of driving drift, and we can see nothing. We go astray early and are briefly lost, and then the compass comes to the rescue and we pick up Big Island and grope our way into Makkovik, arriving in the early afternoon.

George Harp, Moravian Missionary at Makkovik, is as hospitable as his colleagues at Hopedale and Hebron and Nain. The Moravians at these four stations, and Mr. Budgell of Nutak and the Reverend Gillett of Postville, have done much to make this medical work possible in recent years, and it is so comforting to come in out of the dirt and stress of dog team travel when it is bad—as it must often be—to utterly considerate and thoughtful care such as these posts offer.

The work at Makkovik is done in a day and a half, and we leave immediately for Adlavik. My team now is my own from North West River. With my good friend Sam Broomfield driving, it would normally have been a wonderful team. It includes three of my own dogs, big pure white animals with a sentimental nature and a vast affection for the doctor, but, alas, the dog feed shortage has already worked ravages on them. We make Adlavik by twilight, though, and spend the night, leaving in the morning for the American weather station at Tishialuk, which we reach in early afternoon. I am dreaming about a hot bath, but the water supply is frozen, and anyway I must go at once to Luceyville for an operation and some more out-patients work, working until after midnight, and returning to the base in time to get to bed at 2 am. Up again at 6:30 and off as soon as possible for the longest day of the trip.

Our dogs, though thin, are willing and are beautifully handled by the veteran Sam, whom I consider the best driver in Labrador. The going is not good, but we keep at it, past Cape Harrison and Byron's Bay, and then across the great portage separating us from Pottle's Bay, which is an extension of Hamilton Inlet. This is a long run, and we make over 65 miles by my reckoning, leaving Halfway Brook at dusk. This portage, like most of them, is largely barrens, but Halfway Brook is marked by a skirt of woods. The weather is good, and the night is pleasant but very dark, so that we can see little, and we lose the track we are following, fumbling for a time in some scrubby woods and finally dropping down on to Tilt Brook about ten o'clock in pitch dark and not too sure of our bearings.

Sam hears dogs howling, and we turn down the brook much reassured, reaching the "city" of two houses half an hour later. Our dogs are very tired, but I have messages from North West River telling me the hospital is very busy and to hurry back, and the hardship to our dogs must be accepted. It is good to be back on Hamilton Inlet again, even though North West River is still over 140 miles away. From Bluff Head we go along the "ballicators" of piled ice on the shore, with open water outside of us. One of my dogs, Sherry, seemed so ill this morning I was considering shooting him, but he is working again as best he can. All dogs are pitifully thin and weak now, and some of them are just stumbling along. We make Rocky Cove two hours after dark and go right to work, finishing the work at 2 am. We leave at dawn and travel into the bay all day, reaching Wolfreyville in Double Mer Bay at twilight. Thank heavens, there is a little seal blubber here, so we stop for the night and give our dogs some of the fat their bodies have been starved for. The next day they are all sick, but seem to pick up well during the morning and we make Rigolet by 10 am, setting up a clinic in the empty school house and seeing all the patients here by 1:30 pm. Lunch and we leave immediately for Mulliauk, where we spend the night, departing at daylight to catch the early frost, which makes the morning snow hard enough to bear up the dogs and the komatik. By 11 am it has melted again and is bad going, and the air is very soft.

We cross the portage from Mulliauk back to Double Mer to see a girl with a tuberculosis spine and arrange for hospital care for her, first open water, as the ice is unsafe for aircraft now, and indeed unsafe for dog teams in places. We cross Double Mer in a rowboat, leaving our teams on the south side of the bay. After a light lunch we return to the teams, and go up Double Mer to another portage, passing back onto Lake Melville only sixty miles from home.

We spend the night at Valley's Bight, leaving around 4 am to catch the morning frost again. Awful going all day, but we shoot a seal after several tries, and our poor dogs will eat tonight. Sam goes on ahead, hoping to shoot another seal, and I drive the dogs. Once we mire down in deep snow and the komatik stops. The going is so awful that we stop at dusk at a small trapper's tilt along this wooded shore and spend the night, leaving again about 3 am and finding rotten going until we reach Black Point, where we take ice that has drained off along the tidal cracks along shore, and we do better, only occasionally breaking through into a foot of water or slush.

We must go all along ten miles of shore instead of cutting out across three or four miles of bay, but we are in Mulligan Village by noon and the work is done by four o'clock and we leave for North West Islands. We cannot take the portage which is only a couple of miles, for the wet snow here is said to be four feet deep and of the consistency of Irish stew. Remembering that it took us half an hour to cross the three hundred yards of slush at the head of Mulligan Bay, we prefer to go out around the cape, an extra ten miles. I shoot some white partridges on the way, in case there is nothing else in the way of dog feed at North West Islands, but they find us dog feed, and the dogs are contented. The last day or two, although terribly thin, they have been a little better. We leave at dawn to catch the slight frost, which bears the team up until we leave Sabasquasho at nine o'clock, and thereafter we follow along shore and reach North West River at noon, completing about 700 miles of the worst travelling I have ever seen.

We have seen a total of 452 patients and evacuated ten by air. About as many more have had hospitalization arranged for the summer, after the opening of navigation. The total distance travelled has been two or three hundred miles less than usual, because the Easter festivals brought many people into the larger centres and eliminated some long trips up bays. I return to find 19 in-patients at North West River and Miss Smith looking about as tired as I feel. The trip is over, though, and from now on I shall sleep in a bed for a while instead of on kitchen floors or snowbanks, and the change will be welcome.

WINTER MEDICAL PATROL, 1950-51

On March 5, we reported at Goose Bay air base for transportation northward by aircraft. Following its custom, the Royal Canadian Air Force had agreed to fly the Mission doctor north to Hebron so he could begin his northern trip. The idea was to make a one way outward flight and return by dog team, visiting every home and hamlet along the way.

Usually it has been customary for the doctor to hire successive teams on his way southward, but this year a new scheme was to be put into effect. I had received assurances from the Group Captain at Goose that the plane could easily take a dog team along if I wanted to bring my own team north, and the opportunity to take my own driver and our stout team, including three big white huskies which I keep at home, was too good to miss.

We had come across the bay to Goose the previous night through a snowstorm and much new snow. The party included myself, my driver, the Provincial Welfare Officer for the district, who was to make the trip with us, and several patients. These were convalescents from northwards, taking passage home. They would otherwise have had to wait for four months until early July for transportation by water. The American army kindly took them across the 25 miles of ice to Goose Bay in a helicopter, but the rest of us went by team.

On the morning of the 5th, we were ready for takeoff and the big Royal Canadian Air Force Dakota transport on skis was ready for us. Five patients, including a baby, and the three men of the party, nine big husky dogs, the long komatik or sledge, and the medical boxes, luggage, sleeping bags, food for four weeks, guns, ammunition, and snowshoes and the like made a formidable pile on the snow-packed hangar ramp. The aircraft swallowed everything up and would easily have taken a second, similar party. Then came the bellow of engines, the whimpering of nervous dogs, and the familiar sensation of sudden release, and the plane was airborne and climbing above the blue spruce clad Goose Bay hills and the broad white expanse of Grand Lake.

The familiar landscape rolled slowly beneath us, empty and lovely wildernesses of frozen lakes and wooded hills and barren mountain tops, and the woods thinned and gave way to rolling tundra or bare rocks, with only small stands of trees huddled timidly along the river banks. The plane banked steeply and began a long descent through rocky hill tops into Nain, where we were to drop off our patients before proceeding on to Hebron. My dogs, drowsy with lack of oxygen, awoke suddenly, and two of my own began a fight, which was hastily suppressed. The ice was rough, and the Dakota wallowed and pounded on the windrows of hard snow, but it was skillfully handled. The commanding officer of Goose Bay was flying it himself, the veteran of thousands of hours of wartime and bush flying. Group Captain Birchall has been a most courteous and helpful neighbour to the Grenfell Mission and has concerned himself deeply with the welfare of the people of Labrador.

After a few moments at Nain, we took off again for Hebron, and as we flew, patches of cloud gathered. The weather became overcast, and most surprising of all, open patches appeared in the ice below us. More and more of the bays proved broken open, and when we reached Hebron Bay, it looked like summertime, with no ice for many miles and a gentle swell crashing white on the rocks of the harbour mouth. I was summoned to the controls for a conference. Radio communication established that the ice had all broken up and gone out to sea during heavy gale the previous day. There was nowhere to land the aircraft, for the ice which would have been our landing field was gone, and only the gently swinging blue sea spread below us. The land was out of the question, nearly all vertical cliffs, and so landing was impossible. I proposed to the Group Captain that we fly back 80 miles to Nutak post, far enough up a narrow bay so that I was sure that the ice would be unbroken, and the Dakota swung southward. Clouds were rolling in but Nutak was still open, and thank heavens the ice was still strong outside the post, although the fjord had broken up for some 20 miles. Again the long descending whistle and the racing plane, poised with stiffly outspread wings, and the jolt and roll of the uneven ice under our landing gear. The dogs were by now quite blasé and ignored the whole proceedings.

It was, so far as I know, the first time for many years that the bays had broken up in March, and it made travelling difficult all this season for everyone.

March 10. Leaving Nutak after a pleasant visit. Max Budgell, government agent, and his wife made us warmly welcome. Only embarrassment came when they asked where their baby son, whom we had brought north with us, was, and we had to confess that we had left him at Nain, not expecting to land at Nutak. Sunny day when we leave the post, going to Udlik to see patients, and thence to Tissujuk to visit Doctor Wheeler, geologist, who has a winter camp in the area. No one there so we proceed on to house of Lukas Okkuatsiak, fine Eskimo hunter and thoughtful host. House very small, sense of tragedy because Lukas' father, old Lukas, had only just died at St. Anthony due to incurable cancer, and we had to break news. Mr. Davis much interested in breakfast of raw, frozen deer meat offered by our hosts, and joins us in some, which sounds very strange breakfast fare but is actually a delicacy, and far nicer than any of our dehydrated or tinned stuff.

March 11. Travelled all day. Met Sam Lyall coming north from Nain on way to Nutak and he tells us the bays are all open and we will have to go all along shore. Since there are cliffs along shore this means much portaging over high hills or clinging to rocks so as to avoid falling into the sea. Come to the big hill he warned us about, find it a 75% slope for some 400 feet of drop. We take the dogs of all four teams out of harness, and the Eskimos send each in succession, with two chain drags on each runner, thundering down the hill unmanned, and each completes the hazardous journey safely.

Lunch in Korokuluk Brook, during the long climb on to the Kiglapait Mountains. This is a 2,000 foot climb on snowshoes up fairly steep grade, very tiring, but I get up well ahead of dogs. In the mountain tops it is cloudy, and depth perception is difficult—one cannot tell if a rock is 10 feet or

1,000 feet distant. One cannot see below snowshoe, as I find, stepping right off the side of a hill and falling helpless for a time, unable to see the snow in which I am sliding. This produces sense of vertigo. Manage to get off the side of this particular hill, but even in bright light I grope as if in dark, and am glad to get off it safely, for a little bit further on the hill steepens into a sheer cliff, which I was unable to see. Wait at an old abandoned snowhouse until teams catch up with me, and we proceed on towards Webb's Brook, winding through the mountain tops all day. Tiring, but we end up in a rocky gulch at dark, only a few miles from the other side of the mountains and the easy level ice leading to Nain.

The Eskimos who are driving the other two teams build us a snowhouse, a perfectly beautifully made thing glowing softly like an inverted bowl with the radiance of the candles within. The snow walls are transparent to light. Pure frosty radiance within, purifying frost and lovely sheen of walls. Only a small cup of melted ice to go with supper, which is, eccentrically enough, frozen raw meat and frozen mince pie, with a bit of frozen cheese. The water freezes in the snow house, but it is warm and snug in my sleeping bag, and I remember nothing more until my driver calls me to organize breakfast.

At daylight hot tea from the primus stove and we start the long descent downwards for the next few miles and dropping an estimated 2,000 feet. Before noon we are on the ice and before dark at Nain, rather cold and glad to be inside.

March 12 to 15. Working at Nain. Bill and Doris Peacock of the Moravian Missions provide the usual heartwarming Moravian Mission hospitality, assisted by Fred and Marjorie Grubb. The Nain Eskimos provide us with considerable work for a few days, but the Moravian assistance simplifies things greatly and we leave on the morning of the 16th.

March 16. Up the long reaches of Nain Bay and across to Voisey's Bay, where we visit the families at the head of the bay and hurry on, reaching John Edmunds home just after dark and camping for the night. Dehydrated vegetables and partridge for supper, a huge and delectable feast after the bread and tea of most trail-side meals, and off in the morning, stopping only at Kamarsuk for a time. We are far along by twilight, and undertake to follow a portage across ten miles of hills to Shango Bay, a portage none of us have ever crossed, and with a rather uncertain trail to follow. It is pitch dark, and the dogs are tired and sluggish, and we are not sure of the way.

At long last we emerge unexpectedly in David Edmunds's back yard, our dogs getting into a wild tangle with each other and the remnants of the feed that David had put out for his own dogs. Unharnessed and into the snug warmth of old David's cozy home before ten o'clock, with the luxury of a bear skin for a mattress over the kitchen floor to spread the sleeping bag on. I should like to carry one or two, but they are heavy. I have a small cushion mattress of muskox skin, denim covered, which is very helpful sleeping out of doors.

March 19. We reach Davis Inlet in driving snowstorm and poor visibility, and stay at the old Agency, now serving as the Oblate Fathers Jesuit mission to the Davis Inlet Indians. Father Cyr welcomes us with the utmost kindness, and he and Lay Brother Leclerc are the most helpful of hosts with our work. The Lay Brother is one of the strongest men physically on the coast, and he is hewing out a 35-foot boat with an axe, an adze, and a pit saw, working alone for long hours in the cold. The boat will be used to help the Indians fish in the summer.

Father Cyr has already won the respect and affection of everyone who has encountered him for his kindliness and his eagerness to work with the other churches and with all those concerned in the welfare of the land. He chatters Indian with his parishioners, who obviously adore him, and Eskimo with our drivers and French with the Lay Brother and English with us and apologizes that his Dutch was not up to conversing with the Reverend Hettasch of Hopedale, who had visited recently.

March 20. Reach Hopedale after a long hard haul, just after dark. Reverend Siegfried Hettasch and his wife welcome us and provide hot food and snug rooms and arrange for all the sick to be rounded up in the morning. Finished in this large Eskimo village on the morning of the 22nd and we are ready to leave, going up Adlavik, where we stay overnight because of a storm. Here we pick up a small team to help us along, as our two teams are struggling with heavy loads. Sam Broomfield and Julius Ford (of Nain) are both considerate companions and skilled and competent teamsters, and impossible to lose. Now they are joined by Jim Gear, of Adlavik, and the three teams leave for Island Harbour, stopping at a house full of seriously ill Eskimos on the way.

Injured boy, cut with axe, evacuated by the Royal Canadian Air Force. His mother, with tuberculosis spine and pulmonary tuberculosis, we arrange for hospitalization, and the father we provide with extra food allowance from the Department of Welfare. A daughter consults us about adoption of a child, and when the papers are complete we leave, reaching Island Harbour after dark. Here the mother of the house has heart disease and the father is ill, and the woman who helps her with the housework appears to be suffering from tuberculosis. We do what we can to dispose of these cases and proceed at daylight the next day, reaching Postville on the evening of the 25th. Reverend Gillett of the Pentecostal Mission there is my genial host, and this enthusiastic and capable Padre shows me the community sawmill scheme he has set up to provide work, and I attend a service in the church Sunday night.

Labrador in general can be proud of its ministers. The Moravians have led their communities for a century and a half, and the newer United Church and Church of England cooperate with them and with the Oblate Fathers and the Pentecosts, the aggregate being one of strong and devout religious leaders who follow Christ and who live in peace and harmony.

On the 27th we reach Makkovik, after an uneventful trip down Kaipokok Bay, and Reverend Harp entertains us. It will be his last year of service after a lifetime of hard work on the coast, and he will be missed by all who ever met him, as will his witty and capable wife.

March 29. Up the long pass across Monkey Hill, and down the mountain brook on the other side, and we make Lance Grounds, after calling at Adlavik en route. Again we see patients and rest well for a comfortable night with old Sam Jacques.

March 30. This is a long day for we have much ground to cover. We make Luceyville by noon, and the medical work is done as soon as possible. John Thomas Lucey seems hurt that we cannot spend the night and rest in his pleasant little home, but we are in a hurry, for telegrams urge us to hurry and to be ready to depart for New York at the first chance. North West River hospital is full, and we have been sending more patients in by airplane all along the way as we have come, so we hurry on and reach an empty house at Tilt Cove just at dark, to find that there is still a stove there and that it is not too hard to make it comfortable for the night. We have killed meat today, so we have fried partridge and it is delicious.

March 31. A long, long day and the dogs are truly tired, for we have come some 65 or 70 miles when we finally make camp at Tilt Cove Brook, stopping only briefly at Big Brook on the way. Many partridges along the way, and we kill several. It has been a tiresome day, but we are back in Hamilton Inlet and barely 150 miles from home. Sick children, teeth to pull out, chests to listen to, and then the oblivion of the sleeping bag until daylight.

April 1. The dogs play an April Fool's Day joke on us, for Job Oliver volunteers to take me out to Rattler's Bight to see patients, my own heavily loaded teams preceding. We have been joined by Bert Allen, and Julius Ford has turned back on the long trip to Nain. Halfway out across the marshes the dogs slip the bridle and run away, leaving us without even snowshoes on the snow-swept marshes. We go on out to the bight on foot, and sure enough there they are, laughing, their traces tangled but waiting for us.

On past Rocky Cove, where we have lunch and treat patients, and to Ticoralak for the night, where we stay for a comfortable night, leaving at dawn. At Double Mer we arrange hospital care for a patient and proceed to Rigolet where we arrive on April 2, setting up a clinic in the village schoolhouse and clearing away all the patients before midnight, leaving us free to go up the Narrows in the morning. Mr. Davis we leave at Rigolet, doing welfare work, and we are away at dawn, stopping at Mulliauk to see a sick woman, who tragically died at North West River later, our one maternal death in many, many years.

Across bad ice this day, and along the steep ice ridges of the narrows, with the hungry black water racing a few feet away. Once the shelf of ice is so narrow we must cut a groove for one runner, since the path is too narrow for both runners, and one hangs out over the water. I climb the little cliff above and with a seal skin whip lash tied to the komatik keep it from rolling outward into the water, and Sam guides it and encourages the dogs. We pass with a sigh of relief.

Tonight we reach Valley's Bight to find it deserted although the house is unlocked, and we make ourselves at home there after the custom of the land. Up at daylight on bad going, but we find that the foot of wet snow and water on the ice can be avoided by following the big cracks along the shore, where the water has run off. It is now mild and wet, and the whole surface of the ice is covered with a foot or so of blue water or with shell ice and wet slush. The crisp, clean cold of a week or so back is gone and the sun shines hot, sunburning everyone. The dogs noses and eyelids are cracked and swollen with sunburn, and I know from experience how they are feeling. They are very tired after nearly a month of going and most of them are bleeding from their feet, leaving crimson stains on the ice. Only Sherry and Ginger, two of my own three white huskies, are able to work without limping, and do not bleed.

At noon on the 4th we stop 25 miles along the shore, while Sam tries to shoot an elusive little seal on the ice. The dogs find a patch of heather from which the snow has melted and go to sleep on it in the hot sun. I join them, and later Sam returns and I hear him laugh. I wake to find Trigger lying by my knees, and Sherry and Ginger each with a head companionably on my shoulders, the four of us asleep in the drowsy heat. Temperature must be in the high 40s or low 50s, and the sun is scorching. The dogs are gentle, foolish, sentimental creatures and my own are so close to me that sometimes I think I know what is going on in their minds. Furiously jealous of each other, they are an armed guard for my little niece, and the self-appointed guardians of all the children at our end of the village. I would not know that a month later Trigger was to be killed in a fight, beaten because his chain had fouled in a stump and choked him so that he was helpless to defend himself. For now the three are beautiful, ivory white in their heavy winter coats, rippling with strength and grace, frolicking despite their weariness, uncomplaining.

The last night is spent at North West Islands, and here we learn that there is an acute appendicitis awaiting us, so we hurry on at daylight, reaching North West River at noon, a month even on the trail and in time to do our operations, tidy up the patient's records and proceed by helicopter to Goose and thence to New York and the Directors' meeting which Doctor Curtis has asked me to attend.

THE OLD AND THE NEW IN LABRADOR TRAVEL

Almost exactly five years ago today, I was weather-bound at Hebron. I had flown down there from Goose Bay in an Royal Canadian Air Force aircraft, and after seeing the patients there during a lovely March day, I was ready to take my departure by dog team. The weather had turned bad just as the work had been completed, and I remained there several days waiting for the wind to die out and the drifting snow to lighten before starting the long trip—nearly 800 miles—on dog team and on foot, to North West River.

The trips were not without their appeal. The close contact with the people of the coast, in whose homes one stayed over night, the fine drivers and their skillful and ungrudging labour to get the komatik ever southward in spite of every obstacle of weather, surface or bad ice—all these things gave a certain meaning to the difficulty of dog-team travel. For it was difficult, make no mistake about that. There was no story-book dashing over the frozen snow. For four weary weeks one struggled southward through deep snow, in foul weather and over uncertain ice. One toiled up steep portages, and then anxiously brought the heavily loaded komatik down the other side to the sea ice again, endeavouring not to damage it in its headlong career. Or one put on snowshoes and toiled ahead of the dogs in deep snow, trying to break some sort of a trail in which they could obtain sufficient footing to drag the heavily loaded komatik through a choking, bottomless morass of new snow.

Memories crowd to mind. On one portage of three miles, we were five and a half hours to the ice on the other side of the peninsula. During the first passage on snowshoes through the nearly four feet of soft snow, it was impossible to lift one's snowshoes over the soft and sliding stuff, and one shuffled through it, content to have it fall in about one to reduce the depth by a couple of feet. 100 yards of this at a time was all a strong man could manage without being forced by shortness of breath to rest. The next two passages of the same hundred yards of snow left some sort of trail that the dogs could plough through—a trench three feet deep. Then one was ready to break down another hundred yards of it. Up banks and slopes, across ponds where water had risen up through the snow to make four feet of slush, finally down through thick woods where the snow fell by tons from the laden trees, and at last to the level ice again after almost six back-breaking hours, and then our rate of travel rose to a triumphant two miles an hour, so that at last, after fourteen hours of continuous struggle in that day we reached a settler's home. There, near midnight, I arrived too stiff and sore to be able to bend, so that I had to be helped out of my snowshoes. The next day it was blowing and drifting and unfit for travel at all, and well it was, for neither I nor my driver were able to get out of our sleeping bags for several hours, and then only after aching muscles had been rubbed with liniment and we had been helped up.

Those snowshoes! 40 miles of bad going in one day, once, and I remember the blood in my socks when I took off my sealskin boots that night. Frozen bread and margarine that splintered in the extreme cold; raw frozen caribou meat in thick slices, chewed as one walked beside the komatik; bad food that gave me indigestion I have had ever since—and also the best in the homes one visited, gladly and freely given to me as a guest, and kindness so unobtrusive and thoughtful that one was unaware of it. The hostesses that stayed up half the night mending and laundering travel-worn clothing and equipment, the hosts that "happened" to be going your way the next morning and took some of your load; the sense of close comradeship.

Yes, there were compensations. One remembers the night sky, while trying to make some hamlet at midnight, when the Northern Lights are brighter and lovelier than you might ever know if you have seen them only after leaving the electric lights to step outside. They look pallid then, compared to the mighty sweep of marching brilliance you can watch developing through a long evening on the trail. The snug warmth of a snowhouse, the dazzling reflection of candlelight on the glittering snow walls, the drowsy roar of a primus stove and the cheerful smell of steeping tea and thawing hash, and then the luxury of a warm sleeping bag. Somehow going to sleep in a snowhouse was rather nicer than awakening in it, when the dog-harnesses under one's sleeping bag were frozen hard, and one's sealskin boots too, and the cold cut like a knife, and the grey light came in through the thin snow walls bleak and pitiful.

Always it was hard work. Sometimes it was fun, sometimes it was terrible. The companionship was grand, and the men you met and worked with were to be seen in the finest light, at their best. It was in some ways a waste of time, though. For a skilled man, a trained doctor, nothing could have been more absurd than to spend a month at a time on dog teams. The only justification was that there was absolutely no other way to visit the people of the coast for medical work. Therefore it had to be done.

Enter the air age, and everything changes. Today, with a hospital filled with 40 or more sick people, one can hardly leave it for a month. So now, instead of planning and equipping a dog team trip, I call for a plane. The bush pilots are a competent crowd, and a more cheerful and obliging lot one could hardly find. The plane drops in, the medical box is loaded, along with any patients awaiting transport home from the hospital, and one is off. Three hours or so will take me to the most remote settlement in my district. There I can do exactly the same work that I used to do in the dog-team days, and—enormously important—I can actually take those who require medical treatment back to hospital with me. After an overnight stay, we load in the morning and are back—if all goes well—patients, doctor, mail, in a few hours.

But, although the back-break and toil of dog-team travel is over, flying in Labrador or northern Newfoundland is still no sport for fledglings. The weather is changeable, and there is a vast lore of bad ice and good, hard snowdrifts and soft, and a thousand tricks of the trade that determine whether you even get off the ground or not; and having got off, whether you get back safely or end up "wrapped up in a ball" somewhere. There are forced landings on lonely lakes, and long waits for improvement in the weather. Wives and families must endure having you missing for days and speculating on the possible reasons for non-appearance.

There is a perpetual mental arithmetic of miles, weight, passenger urgency, fuel consumption, etc., which must be shared with the pilot if the work is to be done well and if the cost is to be kept down. An error here may cost someone six hundred dollars for a wasted trip, or a trip in which some vital patient is missed and will require an extra special trip. No empty seat must ever be wasted, and one must calculate the costs of deviations from one's course to pick up discharged patients for return to home against the cost of keeping them in hospital until the next plane, etc., etc. And there are errands and commissions and favours to be planned, for the airplane is the only real communication in Labrador today.

A piece of a film projector is needed at one community. Another has had a breakdown of its lighting system and wires to know if we can collect the replacement part at the post office at Goose Bay and bring it. There is insulin for a woman at Davis Inlet and digitalis for a heart case at Makkovik, to be dropped from the passing plane; and always, everywhere, letters and notes for patients and requests for medicine and for advice and help. "Please come quick, and when you come, would you bring a part for a sawmill with you, or the men in town will all be unemployed"—so it goes. It must all be integrated into the utmost use of the available transportation, and the lowest possible cost to the government departments who are paying for it. It is saving lives, though, and it is improving the overall health enormously, and it will be the making of some of these communities.

The ancient problems remain on the coast. The hills over which one struggled in yesteryear still stand, and stretch cruel claws into the skies to tear the unwary aircraft back out of its element. The fog still flows across their shoulders suddenly, without warning or apparent cause, and where yesterday one could make a snowhouse and camp until it cleared, today one must find one's way out of a maze of peaks at 120 miles an hour—and do it at once. The cold was a hardship when one emerged from the warmth of sleeping bag, and it is even more a hardship today, for if the skill and experience of the pilot is not equal to the task, the engine will refuse to start at -35, and if it does not start almost instantly, the battery will be exhausted, and there you will sit until someone comes to the rescue, or until your resourcefulness finds a solution. The bush pilots are nothing if not resourceful, and it is a pleasure to work with them.

Only the other day we left Cartwright at four o'clock in a Norseman aircraft. The local weather was uncertain, but the report for Goose Bay was excellent. There was a patient to be picked up at Rigolet on the way home. The ice was rough at Cartwright, the big engine roared, and the plane went staggering and bounding down the harbour, and then the engine note changed to that triumphant bellow of power which always follows the sudden breaking of contact with either snow or water, and we lifted easily and turned towards Rigolet, 50 miles away. The clouds lay thinly over the frozen land, and visibility was perhaps five miles or more. The frozen ponds and patches of stunted spruce and the wind-scoured rocks unreeled below us, and the aircraft lurched as it crossed the higher hills and turbulent air struck at our wings.

The headwind was more than we had anticipated, and the country passed with alarming slowness. At last we passed over Rigolet and slanted down into the little frozen pond which is their "airport," settling like a tired duck into the deep snow. A dog team was waiting for us with our patient, who had never flown before. She looked doubtfully at the aircraft, but we strapped her into a seat, and again the engine thundered and the aircraft lifted easily in the stiff breeze, skimmed across the tree-tops, and threaded its ascending way through the hilltops into light overcast. The headwind was now violent, and although the airspeed remained the leisurely 110 of a Norseman, the ground went by at little over half that speed. The twilight was upon us, and the hills were blurred and uncertain in the waning light.

We took the north side of Lake Melville, but visibility was down to a couple of miles and finally to even less. There was no turning back. The afternoon's struggle with headwinds had used up much fuel, and the tank indicators all were down near empty. Slowly, too slowly, the hills passed by us, and we could see nothing but the vague whiteness of the frozen bay and the dim contours of the shoreline beneath us. As the light faded, it turned out that the instrument panel light bulb had burned out and the cabin light was turned on in order to see instruments. Fuel remained in one tank, and the level sank steadily. The patient, who had had a brief indoctrination in the comfort and safety of flight, was held in her bucking seat only by her safety belt; her thoughts she wisely kept to herself.

The familiar outlines of the islands near North West River drew slowly near, and we were able to leave the shoreline and strike out directly for our destination. Then the long whistling descent, while the aircraft pitched and shuddered in the turbulent air, and the familiar jolting and banging as it wallowed across the snow drifts to its final rest at the foot of Portage Road.

The lights of home were just coming on, and very warm and inviting they looked—much nicer than the gathering darkness and the snow-covered trees of some cove where we might have landed to spend an uneasy night awaiting daylight and better weather before coming on home.

Things have changed along this coast, but not as much, perhaps, as one might at first suppose. The coast remains the same, and the problems are the same. A valuable new instrument has been added, which makes possible a great deal more work by the available medical personnel. The airplane is a very important part of our total armament, and the difficulties and the toil of dog team days are too recent for us to become very sentimental about the passing of an era.

POISON IVY

This letter was in Dad's papers, and I couldn't resist including it, even though it was written by Grandfather. It gives the reader an idea of some prevailing attitudes at the time and is one of many such examples. Both Harry and Tony were inundated with requests for data and studies on Indigenous populations, and some of them were peculiar to say the least. They always took the time to answer, even if only to say that they couldn't help. In this case the response was a bit more pointed.

Harry L. Paddon, *Maraval*
to Alexander Forbes, *Ramah*

Indian Harbour
20 August 1931

I received your letter with its enclosure from Professor Heinbecker requesting me to treat from fifteen to fifty Indians with virus of Poison Ivy. Research work is always stimulating and there is an old adage that one good turn deserves another. We in this country are troubled from time to time with infections from some virus or bacillus contained in the fat of seals. I enclose a bottle of seal oil and would be much interested and gratified if Professor Heinbecker would inoculate from fifteen to fifty American professors and very kindly tabulate the results. We are familiar with the result of seal infection here just as Professor Heinbecker is with the effects of Poison Ivy on American citizens. I was fortunate enough to secure the services of the Rockefeller Foundation Unit to investigate the Bacteriology of the Seal oil wounds.

The Professor states that he is in no hurry to secure records of the effects of Poison Ivy on Indians, on the other hand, I should like to know the effects of seal oil on American professors with the least possible delay. Immediately on hearing from him the results of his investigation, I will take my chance of dividing my scalp between from fifteen to fifty outraged Indians.

Yours very sincerely, [Harry Paddon]

P.S. I believe there are a number of Indians in the United States. There are no American professors here.

WHALE AUTOPSY

One of Dad's favourite places to stop in the summers was the whaling station at Hawkes Harbour on the south coast of Labrador. The staff was always very welcoming and would put on a great meal. On one occasion, they asked Dad to retrieve the pituitary glad from the depths of one of the whales. (An American university wanted it for research, and it was to be packed in salt and sent off.)

This was an unusual request, and the staff had no idea where to find this particular organ. Dad said he'd have a try and was eventually successful. A few months later he sent this letter to the manager, and it's a great example of his sense of humour.

Hospital Ship *Maraval*
North West River, Labrador

Mr. Larsen
Manager, Polar Whaling Company
Hawkes Harbour, Labrador

Dear Sir:

It has just come to my attention that the *Maraval* failed to render you a bill for the location and removal of the pituitary gland from the depth of one of your whales in early July.

We hope that this delay has not inconvenienced your

cashier.

In the preparation of this account I have been frankly rather puzzled as to just how to make charges. Since the operation was properly a post-mortem examination or autopsy I decided to make charges on this grounds, using the provincial autopsy scale as a criterion.

The province makes payment to the medical profession and to hospital administrations for autopsy of dead body including cranial cavity or examination of any organ in body or cranial cavity at the flat rate of $15.00. Naturally a whale is somewhat outsize for the most literal interpretation of this scale, and I have arbitrarily reached the following conclusion.

The average dead body weighs 67 kg or 150 lbs. Charging for autopsy at the rate $15 per 150 lbs we arrive at a figure of $200 per ton. I am advised that the whale concerned tipped the scale at about 80 tons, which is to say that at $200 per ton the medical services I rendered you should be worth approximately $16,000.00.

For so tremendous an autopsy this seems like a very small figure, but I do not like to make it any higher than stated, as I understand that you are trying to cut down expenses wherever possible, a policy in which I receive the utmost encouragement from the management of my own organization. I therefore submit the following account for your consideration. Of course, if you would like to make an additional slight contribution to the Grenfell Mission for services rendered I should be most happy, on behalf of the directors of the Mission, to accept it and see that it is spent in some worthy Mission enterprise.

To:
The Polar Whaling Company

Services rendered professionally at rate of $15 per average corpse tonnage of 150 lbs.

One whale @80 tons	$16,000.00
Item, Federal Sales Tax 8%	$1,280.00
Item, one package of Kleenex to clean doctor's shoes	$0.12
Item, one bottle toilet water sprinkled over doctor by crew	$0.87
Total	$17,280.99

2% discount for cash within 30 days.

Sincerely
W.A. Paddon, MD
Medical officer, *Maraval*

THE PATIENTS

The story of outdoor surgery is also related in Labrador Doctor, *but this seemed a good place to include a look at post -World War Two medical work in Labrador and northern Newfoundland. Dad was totally devoted to Labrador and his fellow Labradorians, and I think it comes through in this piece.*

The Grenfell Mission was a stop-gap measure which provided health and educational services at a time when governments either couldn't or wouldn't. Not long after Grenfell arrived, he said, "We'll know our work is done when we are no longer needed." It took about 90 years, but the transition was eventually complete, and now health services in northern Newfoundland and Labrador are much the same as in any other remote part of Canada.

In 2012 I was working on a ship that stopped in Makkovik for a few hours. I found myself in the house of Bert Winters who, as a young man, had driven dog teams for dad on a number of occasions. On learning my identity he exclaimed (three times in a row) "your father was some *doctor!" He then proceeded to regale me with stories of a bygone era, and I was transfixed.*

The doctors and nurses of the wartime and post-war Grenfell Mission were an amazing group. Forged with the kind of idealism that is bestowed by wartime experience and all that it demands in terms of self-sacrifice for a greater cause. I am proud to say my parents were a part of this group.

The patients of Labrador must surely have been among the most cooperative and appreciative imaginable. Throughout two generations of my family from 1912 to 1978 and encompassing the Innu, Inuit, and Settler alike they were respectful, trusting, and willing to do whatever they could to cooperate with doctors, nurses and the hospitals. Rarely was treatment refused, and usually for what, to the patient or family concerned, was a hopeless prognosis. In such circumstances they preferred to have the patient die at home and with his or her family present. This was perfectly understandable but of course medical and surgical skills were beginning to develop very fast at the time that my own practice in Labrador began, and ever increasing numbers of patients were recovering instead of dying.

Father had not pressed too hard to admit a child with far advanced tuberculosis, knowing that death was inevitable. But suddenly it became possible to retrieve such cases in hospital and send them home permanently cured. There were many other instances where patients that were considered quite hopeless before were readily curable with antibiotics or surgery. In general the people adapted to the new order, and it was increasingly obvious that the best place to be if you were seriously ill was the hospital. To have your wife or child in the local hospital was not too disturbing, but to have these sent away to St. Anthony—perhaps to die alone far from home—remained a very difficult decision. The bluff kindness and the surgical skill of Doctor Curtis had already convinced many people that St. Anthony was often one's best chance of recovery in certain cases—or one's only chance—but it had been a long way to go, and many had not returned.

With the conquest of tuberculosis by antibiotics, the disfiguring and disabling thoracoplasties and other surgical treatments could at last be abandoned, and indeed most tuberculosis could be treated locally, usually for a stretch in hospital followed by a return home and even to work while still on drug therapy. Although I realized that it was unusual and looked on as bad medicine, I had to take into consideration the needs and way of life of the Inuit, or Innu particularly, and as long as we knew for certain that a reliable nurse was available to see that such patients did indeed get their medications for tuberculosis, we returned them to their homes and got them back to work a good deal earlier than was orthodox, nor did we ever have a single relapse in any such patients. Far better to go back to work earlier, feed your family, and provide for them than to lie in bed worrying about whether they were getting enough food and being provided for by someone else. The patients did indeed faithfully take their medicines and did just as well as those whose doctors clung to the fiction that total rest was somehow beneficial to tuberculosis patients.

The patients were surely the most pleasant and easiest to manage that I have ever seen, regardless of which of the three races they represented. At North West River, of course, there were both Innu and Inuit living in the community, and so patients from further north could talk to friends or relatives in their own language and felt infinitely less isolated because of this.

Their behaviour in hospital was really incredibly good, and they put up with the unfamiliar food, the unavoidably strict regime, and the unpleasant things such as long needles, painful treatments, anaesthetics, and a fairly comprehensive ignorance of what was going on.

I—or my colleagues—endeavoured to keep them fully informed about their ailments in so far as they could understand us, and answered every possible question they put to us. Morning rounds were informal, with a bit of chat and as much information as the patient could absorb and wanted to hear, and so far as I am aware none of us ever made any such hideous blunder as I once heard in St. Luke's Hospital in New York.

The head of the surgical staff pointed to a desperately ill young boy with a staphylococcal bacteremia (staph, germs actually in his bloodstream and multiple large abscesses in and on his body). "Personally," he trumpeted. "I've never seen one of these cases survive!" The look on the lad's face was that of stark despair and anguish. The pretty little Scotch nurse broke the silence. "Doctor," she said. "A very urgent matter has just come up in the ward office, and I must urge you to come there at once, and the rest of you, too."

We trailed after her into the room. "Doctor," she said. "That was the most callous and stupid thing I have ever heard an attending surgeon say in the presence of a patient. It was unprofessional, brutal, and probably wrong in any case. If you ever make a mistake like that again, I'll have you before the Superintendent, and you know what he will do to you!!!" He slunk out muttering something apologetic, and his deputy made his ward rounds for him for some time afterwards. I have never forgotten the incident, and have reminded myself hundreds of times of the dangers of talking over a patient.

In that case the nurse and I went back to Bobby Engels—rounds had been terminated by common assent. We both pointed out to him that he had just been put on the newest and most powerful antibiotic, sulfathiazole—which was proving very successful—and that he was not going to die, but would instead probably walk out the front door of St. Luke's under his own power in the next few weeks. In fact it took the next six weeks, for he had been desperately emaciated and toxic, but walk out he did, completely recovered, and his recovery probably began then, five minutes after he received his death sentence.

With government help, we built five little houses down near the shore of Lake Melville, reserved for the Inuk husband or wife, so that they could be discharged from hospital to live with spouse—and yes, children—for once they were on the three main antitubercular drugs, there was little danger of infection amongst the rest of the family. Aside from being much cheaper than keeping the patient in a hospital bed, it was infinitely pleasanter, and the couple could be together again. All of this, together with the extended hospital ship cruises and the dog team patrols—to be followed by medical aviation—brought us closer to the people, both native and settler. That closeness was enhanced by the visits of the doctor to the communities, and to his sharing of home and food in Native homes along the way.

No house could have been more gracious or warm hearted than those of the Settlers and the Inuit. While one slept—for it was usual to retire reasonably early if the snowshoe travel for example had been strenuous—busy hands repaired damage to clothing, boots and mitts, stayed up to bake a fresh loaf for the doctor and teamster, or anything else that was needed. There was, of course, a strong family aspect to this, for most such families had met my brothers and myself when we were children, and remembered both my father and mother personally, and were pleased that I had chosen to continue his work. After my marriage they knew all about Sheila, who had nursed some of them, and as housekeeper in the hospital for a time, had ample opportunity to talk to the patients in hospital.

They accepted surgery cheerfully and took it for granted that this was essential. For other than the bread-and-butter surgery such as appendices, fractures of the usual sort, Caesarean sections, and the occasional emergency procedures which simply could not be transferred to the larger hospital because of non-flyable weather, we were more than glad to transfer them to Gordon Thomas. Sometimes the patient would flatly refuse to be any further from home than North West River. This often meant a somewhat longer stay away from home, which the women particularly wanted to avoid in most cases. We began to reduce the surgery slowly and send more and more patients south as air transport became more extensive. The fact that good orthopaedics was available there was another strong attraction to St. Anthony, though the Native people, particularly, generally wanted their surgery at North West River if possible.

In a practice as unusual as this, and often with no alternative to taking on many surgical procedures, we operated on several hundred patients, some of them grave emergencies, and we lost several. One or two were damned-if-I-do-and-damned-if-I-don't situations that failed, and to lose such a patient was a crushing blow in a community which looked to me to be right all of the time.

Still, we performed hundreds of major operations with no mishap, and our patients had the utmost faith in us. Never once did I ever have the slightest recrimination from any family in the north. It was taken for granted that one had done one's best, and that was that. As transport became better and more planes were available, we could move patients more easily, and did so, and in time we reduced our major operations substantially. Sometimes the demand that patients be transferred to St. Anthony put one in a difficult spot, for the weather was often unfit for flying. On one occasion it was insisted that I transfer a case of eclampsia to St. Anthony (not by Doctor Thomas, who was away at the time), and I flatly refused because the weather was bad and expected to get worse, and a single-engine bush plane was no help whatever if it were forced down en route by weather. I promised to send the patient when weather improved or alternatively to get her to St. John's. I once spent 19 days in an isolated village waiting for the weather to improve, and am very glad that we did not have a woman with eclampsia to deal with. In the case cited, we hung on to the patient, treated her as we had always treated this ailment and saw her improve notably, and in due course she was sent to St. Anthony in good flying weather and delivered there uneventfully.

Nonetheless, the loss of a surgical patient—or any patient—is a shocking enough occasion anywhere, and far more so in the small villages of the Labrador where one has been known since childhood, and I am deeply grateful for the kindness and the faith they offered me. No one ever questioned the death, and I was trusted implicitly.

One does one's best, and must lose a life from time to time regardless of skill or dedication. Looking back on the past, I think I was lucky to be trained on a good surgical service in New York and was able to save a considerable amount of pain, suffering and life itself in Labrador in the late '40s. Doctor Curtis expressed anxiety about surgery at North West River, suggesting that I should send these cases to the Royal Canadian Air Force. Little did he know that in the frequent absence of any surgeon at Goose Bay, I was called on by the commanding officer to do surgical procedures for the Air Force and did so several times. The Air Force was pleased, so were the patients, and it seemed the least I could do after the generous help they had given to the Grenfell Association's work.

The three peoples of Labrador were completely kind to me in every way, offered me complete cooperation, and appeared to have confidence in the North West River Hospital and the medical services provided. There were people in Happy Valley working for the base who considered the services we offered there inadequate, and so they were, but no one else was willing to offer them anything. Gradually we built a hospital, later a much larger and more sophisticated one, finally provided a surgeon, a good anaesthetist, and other useful staff members. Until this was complete, I usually did surgery twice a week at Happy Valley, the civilian part of Goose Bay.

One of the differences between medicine or surgery in the North and that in more conventional surroundings is the occasionally bizarre setting for such procedures. Diagnoses, at least the taking of histories and physical examinations, can follow more orthodox practice, though the presence of the entire family and relatives sometimes proves unnerving to a doctor unused to this. The lack of privacy for examinations and interviews is unsettling, and the fact that few Inuit or Innu were fluent in English and I was virtually ignorant of Inuktitut and Innu made interpreters necessary—if indeed I could find one. But it was the procedures that sometimes taxed one's ingenuity and aplomb. A few illustrations might help.

It was a village called New Ferolle, in northern Newfoundland, where I set my own record for dentistry. The office was someone's living room. The "waiting room" was the kitchen, but in the course of time that day, the two rooms seemed to be full of people from both categories. Since there had apparently been no dentist in the area for most of World War Two, there was a large backlog of dental sufferers, so I undertook to dispose of the diagnoses and treatments or other arrangements during the fore-noon and most of the afternoon, starting then on the people who wanted dental extractions. I had become reasonably proficient at this, but was rather appalled at the size of the dental clinic. Patients were taken in blocks of half a dozen with problems in their lower jaws first, and I did three at a time, blocking the nerve supply to the lower jaw with local anaesthetic and then trying to do each in succession in the same order, taking out the offending teeth in the anaesthetized area.

This meant working fast, before the patients already injected found their anaesthesia starting to wear off. It worked well, however, and certainly speeded things up. Upper jaw anaesthesia works faster. One could generally proceed almost immediately with the extraction. By the time of a halt for an evening meal, there were some 75 teeth in a bucket, and some 30 patients had cheerfully paid me 25 cents for each tooth. After something to eat, the work started again, and it was not until 2 am that I had removed a day's total of 173 teeth. Let me hasten to add that many of these were badly decayed and very loose, and the figure was adjusted to 150 genuine extractions and 23 mere roots or partial teeth which were already tottering. Many of the others were quite substantial, and the patients concerned got their 25 cents worth of treatment and were well pleased. There was a trail of blood in the snowy path from the door the next morning leading away from the house when we left it at 6 am for the day's work.

Occasionally my chief, Doctor Curtis, suggested I was turning into a dentist and should attend to more orthodox medicine and surgery, but he was willing to listen to my case, which was that if a new doctor showed himself able to relieve severe pain quickly and painlessly in this way, he would have made many friends and achieved a reputation for competence. This proved very true the following year in Labrador, where most people had not seen me since I was a child there, and particularly the isolated Settlers and the Native people were waiting to assess the new doctor.

Though it seemed a waste of time in one sense, with so much malnutrition, tuberculosis, and untreated illness of many kinds in Labrador, the patients who found the new doctor willing to do anything to relieve pain and able to do it well soon came to him with complaints they would otherwise have kept to themselves. The dental cases who were thus relieved were the ones who first dared to send their wives and children away to the hospital when the hospital ship *Maraval* turned up the next summer. Both friendship and confidence in the doctor were increased, understandably, by his interest in any pain or disability, of whatever nature.

In the past, too often people who had incurable illnesses or very advanced tuberculosis were carted off to hospital far to the south to die in loneliness and isolation in a hospital where no one spoke Inuktitut or Innu. This seemed a good time to start evacuating hospital cases only when it was clear that they would benefit, and in two or three years the attitude towards hospital care altered drastically for the better in the more northerly villages and among the North West River Innu.

One more episode is worth presenting, because apart from its slightly bizarre setting, it says something about the Inuk as a patient. It happened in the winter of 1948 or '49 and certainly caught me off guard. With two Inuit drivers and a large dog team we were on our way north from Nain to Hebron. It was a nice, relatively mild March day, temperature perhaps around zero, somewhat overcast, and we had just climbed a rather long hill on our shortcut from one frozen inlet to the next one. A good deal of our way was on level sea ice, but we portaged at times to save extra miles.

Just as we reached the summit, our dogs began

to run and we heard the sounds of another team, which in fact met us almost exactly on the summit. There was a single figure on the komatik, who waved us back, for his dogs, like most of them, loved a fight with a strange team. Finally the yelping and squealing and the crack of the long sealskin whips subsided, and the two teams were lying on the snow, panting from the climb and relatively peaceful again. The Inuk came over and spoke in his own language. One of my drivers spoke a little English, and I knew a few of the more clinical Inuktitut words. The told us he had had pain, with no relief, for over a month.

There was a very bad place over his left shoulder blade, swollen, very painful, weeping liquid. He hadn't been able to get a real sleep for weeks and was on his way to Nain to see me, for he had heard on radio telephone that I was North. Asked to show us his problem, he suddenly removed his deerskin kulituk or parka. Except for a large bundle of rag strapped over his shoulder and around his chest, he was naked to the waist, for the kulituk is so warm that underwear is seldom necessary. It was, as I say, around zero, and there was perhaps a five- or ten-mile breeze on the hilltop. I could not ask him to turn around and go back, and it would be no good for him to go south.

We had a brass primus stove, a sort of blowtorch which burned kerosene, one of the white man's contributions to the Inuit which had been of real value to travellers, and my drivers got it out at my request, pumped it up and lit it, and melted a kettle of snow over it. The patient had replaced his kulituk and was watching with real interest. From my medical box we took a sterilized 30 mL syringe and a couple of long needles and a bottle of Novocaine tablets, plus knife, sterile gauze (a gaudy orange from its antiseptic impregnation), elastic adhesive which I put under my own parka to keep warm and sticky until needed, and other goodies of my trade. Pulling out the plunger, one could then put in the correct number of Novocaine tablets and replace the plunger and twist it around, grinding them to powder. By now the kettle was boiling, so all that was necessary was to suck up the 30 mL of boiling water through the needle, and we had a syringe full of strong local anaesthetic.

Inspection of the shoulder had revealed a huge carbuncle perhaps five inches in diameter and an inch high, with many draining openings. The solution was injected into and under the skin in a circle along the outer edge of this frightful object. In moments, the patient announced that his pain was gone, and he did in fact get good anaesthesia, so all that was left to do was to make two long slashes in it, each about three inches long, in a cross, then dig out all that lay within with a gloved finger and pack the very large empty space that was left with medicated gauze. Then a large dressing pad and my warmed-up adhesive tape.

Exposed perhaps ten minutes to below-zero wind, the patient was looking a little blue with cold, but on went the warm parka, and he drew a deep breath. "Nakummek," he said, which seemed to sum up the whole situation. I asked my drivers to make some tea with the remaining hot water, which we shared while we told the patient how to manage his wound. The patient decided to go on to Nain to trade. He said he felt fine, and although he probably didn't after the Novocaine wore off, he couldn't have felt any worse than before surgery. Repeatedly he shook my hand, and repeated, "Nakummek, nakummek," before heading south. Our next meeting would not be for a year and a half, when he came aboard *Maraval.* I did not recognize him, so with a broad smile he pulled off his shirt and showed me a little white cross, two linear white lines which I recognized as the scars of the two big slashes I had made in his shoulder. He said he had had no further pain at all, and it had closed up in two or three weeks.

It was hard not to reflect on my fellow interns at St. Luke's hospital in New York, now probably all well-established surgeons in the seven years since I had last seen them, with their offices in suitable parts of the city, their regular surgical meetings and alumni dinners and the like. What, one had to wonder, would they have thought of such a crude and improbable surgical procedure? Anyway, any time I get delusions about my surgical role, I have only to remember the curious and sometimes ridiculous things that happened to me.

ACKNOWLEDGEMENTS

I would like to thank those who made this publication possible. Brack and Brine is Labrador's first publishing company and, as such, they are getting both the history and ongoing story of my homeland out to a curious audience. Mark Turner and Morgen Mills put a huge amount of time and effort into the book. My part was easy by comparison.

I'd also like to thank Andy Jones, Holly Hogan, and Marnie Parsons for taking the time to read it and provide a quote. The staff at The Rooms Provincial Archives helped a lot and, to anyone looking for historical material, I highly recommend this resource.

Thanks to Kimmy, Liz, Mike, Tom and cousin Mike for your contributions and suggestions. Also to Tommy Watt.

Sheila Fortescue gets a taste of Newfoundland winter on board the schooner *Cluett*, off Bonne Bay in November 1949.

Surgeon Lieutenant Commander Tony Paddon. This portrait was taken sometime during World War Two.

SOURCES

PART I–SHEILA PADDON REMEMBERS

All chapters in Part I are transcribed from Dave Paddon's interviews with Sheila Paddon.

PART II–*LABRADOR DOCTOR*, EXPANDED

"Log of *Maraval*, 1946" is reproduced from *Among the Deep Sea Fishers,* January, April, and July 1947.

"Something in the Air" is reproduced from *Among the Deep Sea Fishers,* January 1946.

"Liberator, a Gift from Above" is by Dave Paddon, based on Tony Paddon's *Labrador Doctor* and conversations with family.

"Butter and Snow House Call" is by Dave Paddon, based on a story from Tony Paddon and conversation with Tommy Watt.

"The Old and the New in Labrador Travel" is reproduced from *Among the Deep Sea Fishers,* July 1956.

All other chapters are drawn from Dave Paddon's original transcriptions of Tony Paddon's personal papers.

PEOPLE AND PLACES

ABOUT THE AUTHOR

Dave Paddon is well-known across Newfoundland and Labrador for his storytelling and recitations. This is his ninth book. He can be found operating the English Harbour Arts Centre with his wife, Kim, regaling audiences at the Crow's Nest Officers Club in St. John's, or anywhere folks appreciate a good yarn.

Brack and Brine publishes beautiful books
that matter to the North.

SEPARATION POINT

Michael Friis Johansen

a Labrador crime thriller

(fiction, forthcoming 2025)

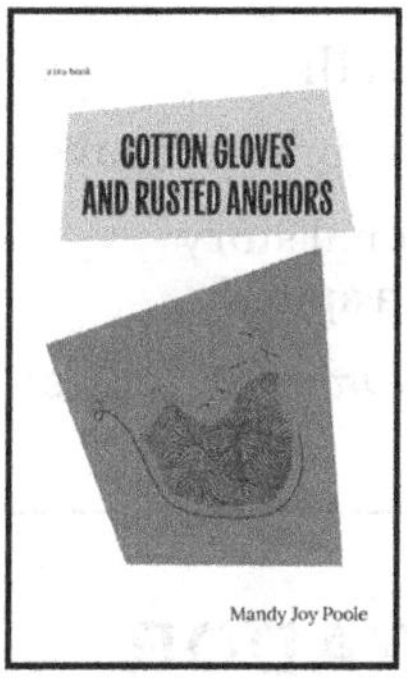

COTTON GLOVES AND RUSTED ANCHORS

Mandy Ford

poetry from an emerging NunatuKavut voice

(forthcoming 2025)

IN THE SHADOW OF TUNGUSUAK

Chris Buckley

a true story of two brothers and adventure in the Torngat Mountains

2025 Foreword INDIES Silver Winner